Django 1.0 Web Site Development

Build powerful web applications, quickly and cleanly, with the Django application framework

Ayman Hourieh

PUBLISHING

BIRMINGHAM - MUMBAI

Django 1.0 Web Site Development

First published: March 2009

Production Reference: 1040309

Published by Packt Publishing Ltd.
32 Lincoln Road
Olton
Birmingham, B27 6PA, UK.

ISBN 978-1-847196-78-1

www.packtpub.com

Cover Image by Raghuram Ashok (raghuram@iiitb.ac.in)

Credits

Author

Ayman Hourieh

Reviewer

Patrick Chan

Senior Acquisition Editor

Douglas Paterson

Development Editor

Ved Prakash Jha

Technical Editor

Darshana D. Shinde

Copy Editor

Sneha M. Kulkarni

Indexer

Hemangini Bari

Production Editorial Manager

Abhijeet Deobhakta

Editorial Team Leader

Abhijeet Deobhakta

Project Team Leader

Lata Basantani

Project Coordinator

Rajashree Hamine

Proofreader

Cathy Cumberlidge

Production Coordinator

Aparna Bhagat

Cover Work

Aparna Bhagat

About the author

Ayman Hourieh holds a bachelor's degree in Computer Science. He joined the engineering team at Google in January 2008. Prior to that, he worked with web application development for more than two years. In addition, he has been contributing to several open source projects such as Mozilla Firefox. Ayman also worked as a teaching assistant in Computer Science courses for one year. Even after working with a variety of technologies, Python remains Ayman's favorite programming language. He found Django to be a powerful and flexible Python framework that helps developers to produce high-quality web applications in a short time.

I would like to thank my wife, Nadia, for all her help in writing this book. Not only did she provide support and motivation, but she also helped me greatly in proofreading and testing. I would also like to thank my mother and father for their continuous support and encouragement.

About the reviewer

Patrick Chan is an analyst programmer with Australia Post. He volunteers with Computer Bank, a not-for-profit organization that recycles donated computers and distributes them to disadvantaged individuals and community groups.

He is currently involved in DjangoDB, a Django project that would upgrade Computer Bank's inventory system by allowing Computer Bank staff to manage its customer records, computer inventory, and transactions. DjangoDB would feature an improved interface with new features, such as enabling users to check for availabilities of computers and generate reports over the Web.

Table of Contents

Preface

Django is a high-level Python web application framework designed to support the development of dynamic web sites, web applications, and web services. It is designed to promote rapid development and clean, pragmatic design. Therefore, it lets you build high-performing and elegant web applications quickly.

In this book you will learn about employing this MVC web framework, which is written in Python—a powerful and popular programming language. The book emphasizes utilizing Django and Python to create a Web 2.0 bookmark-sharing application, with many common features found in the Web 2.0 sites these days. The book follows a tutorial style to introduce concepts and explain solutions to problems. It is not meant to be a reference manual for Python or Django. Django will be explained as we build features throughout the chapters, until we realize our goal of having a working Web 2.0 application for storing and sharing bookmarks.

I sincerely hope that you will enjoy reading the book as much as I enjoyed writing it. And I am sure that by its end, you will appreciate the benefits of using Python and Django for your next project. Both Python and Django are powerful and simple, and provide a robust environment for rapid development of your dynamic web applications.

What this book covers

Chapter 1 gives you an introduction to MVC web development frameworks, and explains why Python and Django are the best tools to achieve the aim of this book.

Chapter 2 provides a step-by-step guide to installing Python, Django, and an appropriate database system so that you can create an empty project and set up the development server.

Chapter 3 creates the main page so that we have an initial view and a URL. You will learn how to create templates for both the main page and the user page. You will also write a basic set of data models to store your application's data..

Chapter 4 is where the application really starts to take shape, as user management is implemented. Learn how to log users in and out, create a registration form, and allow users to manage their own accounts by changing email or password details.

Chapter 5 explores how to manage your growing bank of content. Create tags, tag clouds, and a bookmark submission form, all of which interact with your database. Security features also come into play as you learn how to restrict access to certain pages and protect them against malicious input.

Chapter 6 enables you to enhance your application with AJAX and jQuery, since users can now edit entries in place and do live searching. Data entry is also made easier with the introduction of auto-completion.

Chapter 7 shows you how to enable users to vote and comment on their bookmark entries. You will also build a popular bookmarks page.

Chapter 8 focuses on the administration interface. You will learn how to create and customize the interface, which allows you to manage content and set permissions for users and groups.

Chapter 9 will give your application a much more professional feel through the implementation of RSS feeds and pagination.

Chapter 10 tackles social networks providing the "social" element of your application. Users will be able to build a friend network, browse the bookmarks of their friends, and invite their friends to join the web site.

Chapter 11 covers extending and deploying your application. You will also learn about advanced features, including offering the site in multiple languages, managing the site during high traffic, and configuring the site for a production environment.

Chapter 12 takes a brief look at the additional Django features that have not been covered elsewhere in the book. You will gain the knowledge required to further develop your application and build on the basic skills that you have learned throughout the book.

Who this book is for

This book is for web developers who want to learn how to build a complete site with Web 2.0 features, using the power of a proven and popular development system—Django—but do not necessarily want to learn how a complete framework functions in order to do this. Basic knowledge of Python development is required for this book, but no knowledge of Django is expected.

Conventions

In this book, you will find a number of styles of text that distinguish between different kinds of information. Here are some examples of these styles, and an explanation of their meaning.

Code words in text are shown as follows: "We can include other contexts through the use of the `include` directive."

A block of code will be set as follows:

```
{% extends "base.html" %}
{% block title %}User Registration{% endblock %}
{% block head %}User Registration{% endblock %}
{% block content %}
<form method="post" action=".">
  {{ form.as_p }}
  <input type="submit" value="register" />
</form>
{% endblock %}
```

When we wish to draw your attention to a particular part of a code block, the relevant lines or items will be shown in bold:

```
import os
from django.conf.urls.defaults import *
from bookmarks.views import *
site_media = os.path.join(
  os.path.dirname(__file__), 'site_media'
)
urlpatterns = patterns('',
  (r'^$', main_page),
  (r'^user/(\w+)/$', user_page),
  (r'^login/$', 'django.contrib.auth.views.login'),
  (r'^logout/$', logout_page),
  (r'^site_media/(?P<path>.*)$', 'django.views.static.serve',
    {'document_root': site_media}),
)
```

Any command-line input or output is written as follows:

```
$ django-admin.py startproject django_bookmarks
```

New terms and **important words** are shown in bold. Words that you see on the screen, in menus or dialog boxes for example, appear in our text like this: "clicking the **Next** button moves you to the next screen".

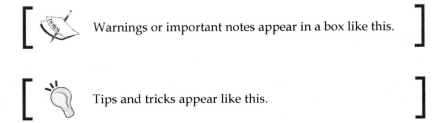

Warnings or important notes appear in a box like this.

Tips and tricks appear like this.

Reader feedback

Feedback from our readers is always welcome. Let us know what you think about this book—what you liked or may have disliked. Reader feedback is important for us to develop titles that you really get the most out of.

To send us general feedback, simply drop an email to feedback@packtpub.com, and mention the book title in the subject of your message.

If there is a book that you need and would like to see us publish, please send us a note in the **SUGGEST A TITLE** form on www.packtpub.com or email suggest@packtpub.com.

If there is a topic that you have expertise in and you are interested in either writing or contributing to a book, see our author guide on www.packtpub.com/authors.

Customer support

Now that you are the proud owner of a Packt book, we have a number of things to help you to get the most from your purchase.

Downloading the example code for the book

Visit http://www.packtpub.com/files/code/6781_Code.zip to directly download the example code.

The downloadable files contain instructions on how to use them.

Errata

Although we have taken every care to ensure the accuracy of our contents, mistakes do happen. If you find a mistake in one of our books—maybe a mistake in text or code—we would be grateful if you would report this to us. By doing so, you can save other readers from frustration, and help us to improve subsequent versions of this book. If you find any errata, please report them by visiting http://www.packtpub.com/support, selecting your book, clicking on the **let us know** link, and entering the details of your errata. Once your errata are verified, your submission will be accepted and the errata added to any list of existing errata. Any existing errata can be viewed by selecting your title from http://www.packtpub.com/support.

Piracy

Piracy of copyright material on the Internet is an ongoing problem across all media. At Packt, we take the protection of our copyright and licenses very seriously. If you come across any illegal copies of our works in any form on the Internet, please provide us with the location address or website name immediately so that we can pursue a remedy.

Please contact us at copyright@packtpub.com with a link to the suspected pirated material.

We appreciate your help in protecting our authors, and our ability to bring you valuable content.

Questions

You can contact us at questions@packtpub.com if you are having a problem with any aspect of the book, and we will do our best to address it.

1
Introduction to Django

Welcome! This book is about Django, an open source web framework that enables you to build clean and feature-rich web applications with minimal time and effort. Django is written in Python, a general purpose language that is well-suited for developing web applications. Django loosely follows a model-view-controller design pattern, which greatly helps in building clean and maintainable web applications.

This chapter gives you an overview of the technologies used in this book. The chapters that follow will take you through a tutorial for building a social bookmarking application from the group using Django.

In this introduction, you will read about the following:

- The MVC pattern in web development
- Why we should use Python
- Why we should use Django
- The history of Django

MVC pattern in web development

Web development has made great progress during the last few years. It began as a tedious task that involved using a protocol called **Common Gateway Interface (CGI)** for interfacing external programs with the web server. The CGI applications used standard I/O facilities available to the C programming language in order to manually parse user input and produce page output. In addition to being difficult to work with, CGI required a separate copy of the program to be launched for each request. This used to quickly overwhelm servers.

Next, scripting languages were introduced to web development, and this inspired developers to create more efficient technologies. Languages such as Perl and PHP quickly made their way into the world of web development. As a result, common web tasks such as cookie handling, session management, and text processing became much easier. Although scripting languages included libraries to deal with day-to-day web-related tasks, they lacked unified frameworks, as libraries were usually disparate in design, usage, and conventions. Therefore, the need for cohesive frameworks arose.

A few years ago, the **model-view-controller** (**MVC**) pattern for web-based applications was introduced. This software engineering pattern separates data (model), user interface (view), and data-handling logic (controller) so that one can be changed without affecting the others. The benefits of this pattern are obvious. With it, designers can work on the interface without worrying about data storage or management. Developers are able to program the logic of data handling without getting into the details of presentation. As a result, the MVC pattern quickly found its way into web languages, and serious web developers started to embrace it in preference to previous techniques.

The following diagram illustrates how each of the components of the MVC pattern interacts with each other to serve a user request:

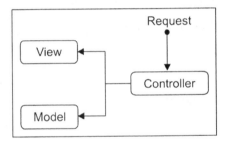

Why Python?

Python is a general purpose programming language. Although it is used for a wide variety of applications, Python is very suitable for developing web applications. It has a clean and elegant syntax. It is supported by a large library of standard and contributed modules, which covers everything from multi-threading to the zipping of files. The language's object-oriented model is especially suited for MVC style development.

Sooner or later, performance will become a major concern with web projects. Python's runtime environment shines here, as it is known to be fast and stable. Python supports a wide range of web servers through modules, including the famous Apache. Furthermore, it is available for all the major platforms: UNIX/ Linux, Windows, and Mac. Python also supports a wide array of database servers, but you won't have to deal directly with them. Django provides a unified layer of access to all available database engines, as we will see later.

Python is a free software that you can download and freely use from `http://python.org/`. You are even allowed to distribute it without having to pay any fees. Access to the source code is available to those who want to add features or fix bugs. As a result, Python enjoys a large community of developers who quickly fix bugs and introduce new features.

Python is very easy to learn, and it is being adopted in many universities as the first programming language to be taught. Although this book assumes working knowledge of Python, advanced features will be explained as they are used. If you want to refresh your Python knowledge, you are recommended to read the official Python tutorial available at `http://python.org/doc/` before continuing with this book.

To sum up, Python was chosen over many other scripting languages for this book. The reasons are:

- A clean and elegant syntax
- A large standard library of modules that covers a wide range of tasks
- Extensive documentation
- A mature runtime environment
- Support for standard and proven technologies such as Linux and Apache

 If you want to learn more about Python and its features, these are two excellent sources: the official Python web site at `http://python. org/` and the Python book *Dive Into Python* (freely available at `http://www.diveintopython.org/`).

Why Django?

Since the spread of the MVC pattern into web development, Python has provided quite a few choices when it comes to web frameworks such as Django, TurboGears, and Zope. Although choosing one out of many can be confusing initially, having several competing frameworks can only be a good thing for the Python community. That's because it drives the development of all the frameworks further and provides a rich set of options to choose from.

Django is one of the available frameworks for Python, so the question is: What sets it apart to become the topic of this book, and what makes it popular in the Python community? The next subsections will answer these questions by providing an overview of the main advantages of Django.

Tight integration between components

First of all, Django provides a set of tightly integrated components. All of these components have been developed by the Django team. Django was originally developed as an in-house framework for managing a series of news-oriented web sites. Later, its code was released on the Internet, and the Django team continued its development using the open source model. Because of its roots, Django's components were designed for integration, reusability, and speed from the start.

Object-Relational Mapper

Django's database component, the **Object-Relational Mapper** (**ORM**), provides a bridge between the data model and the database engine. It supports a large set of database systems, and switching from one engine to another is a matter of changing a configuration file. This gives the developer great flexibility if a decision is made to change from one database engine to another.

Clean URL design

The URL system in Django is very flexible and powerful. It lets you define patterns for the URLs in your application and define Python functions to handle each pattern. This enables developers to create URLs that are both user and search engine friendly.

Automatic administration interface

Django comes with an administration interface that is ready to be used. This interface makes the management of your application's data a breeze. It is also highly flexible and customizable.

Advanced development environment

In addition, Django provides a very nice development environment. It comes with a lightweight web server for development and testing. When the debugging mode is enabled, Django provides very thorough and detailed error messages with a lot of debugging information. All of this makes isolating and fixing bugs very easy.

Multilingual support

Django supports multilingual web sites through its built-in internationalization system. This can be very valuable for those working on web sites with more than one language. The system makes translating the interface a very simple task.

The standard features expected of a web framework are all available in Django. These include the following:

- A template and text filtering engine with simple, but extensible syntax
- A form generation and validation API
- An extensible authentication system
- A caching system for speeding up the performance of applications
- A feed framework for generating RSS feeds

Even though Django does not provide a JavaScript library to simplify working with AJAX, choosing one and integrating it with Django is a straightforward matter, as we will see in later chapters.

So to conclude, Django provides a set of integrated and mature components with excellent documentation at `http://www.djangoproject.com/documentation/`, thanks to its large community of developers and users. With Django available, there has never been a better time to start learning a web development framework!

History of Django

Django started as an internal project at the Lawrence Journal-World newspaper in 2003. Often, the web development team there had to implement new features or even entire applications within hours. Therefore, Django was created to meet the fast deadlines of journalism web sites, while at the same time keeping the development process clean and maintainable. By the summer of 2005, Django became mature enough to handle several high-traffic sites, and the developers decided to release it to the public as an open source project. The project was named after the jazz guitarist, Django Reinhardt.

Now that Django is an open source project, it has gathered developers and users from all over the world. Bug fixes and new features are introduced on a daily basis, and the original development team keeps an eye on the whole process to make sure that Django remains what it is meant to be—a web framework for building clean, maintainable, and reusable web applications.

Summary

Web development has made large leaps of progress over the last few years. The advent of scripting languages, web frameworks, and AJAX made rapid development of web applications possible and easier than ever. This book takes you through a tutorial for building a Web 2.0 application using two hot technologies: Python and Django. The application allows users to store and share bookmarks. Many of the exciting Web 2.0 applications will be explained and developed throughout this book.

In the next chapter, we will set up our development environment by installing the necessary software, and get a feel for Django by creating our first application.

2
Getting Started

Python and Django are available for multiple platforms. In this chapter, we will see how to set up our development environment on UNIX/Linux, Windows, and Mac OS X. We will also see how to create our first project and connect it to a database.

We will learn about the following topics in this chapter:

- Installing Python
- Installing Django
- Installing a database system
- Creating your first project
- Setting up the database
- Launching the development server

Installing the required software

Our development environment consists of Python, Django, and a database system. There are many different database systems available. In this book, we will be using a system known as SQLite. In the following section, we will see how to install the necessary software packages.

Installing Python

Django is written in Python, so the first step in setting up our development environment is to install Python. Python is available for a variety of operating systems, and installing it is not very different from installing any other software package. The procedure depends on your operating system.

You will need a recent version of Python. Django requires Python 2.3 or higher. The latest version of Python, at the time of writing, is 2.5.

We will now look at the installation process for each operating system.

Installing Python on Windows

Python has a standard installer for Windows users. You will need to go to `http://www.python.org/download/` and download the latest version of Python. Next, double-click the `.exe` file and follow the installation instructions. The graphical installer will guide you through the installation process and create shortcuts to Python executables in the **Start** menu.

Once the installation has been done, we need to add the Python directory to the system path so that we can access Python while using the command prompt. To do this, open the **Control Panel**, double-click on the **System** icon, go to the **Advanced** tab, and click the **Environment Variables** button. A new dialog box will open. Select the variable **Path** from the **System variable** section, and append the path where you have installed Python. (The default path is usually `c:\PythonXX`, where XX is your Python version. So if you have Python 2.5, you should append `c:\Python25`.) Don't forget to separate the new path from the one before it with a semicolon.

If you want to test your installation, open the **Run** dialog, type `python`, and hit *Enter*. The Python interactive shell should open.

Installing Python on UNIX/Linux

If you are using Linux or UNIX, the chances are that you already have Python installed. To check, open a terminal, type `python` and hit *Enter*. If you see the Python interactive shell, then you already have Python installed:

```
Python 2.5.1 (r251:54863, May 2 2007, 16:56:35)
[GCC 4.1.2 (Ubuntu 4.1.2-0ubuntu4)] on linux2
Type "help", "copyright", "credits" or "license" for more information.
>>>
```

The first line of the output indicates the version installed on your system (2.5.1 here).

If you receive an error message instead of seeing the output, or have an old version of Python, you should read on.

UNIX and Linux users are recommended to install and update Python through the system package manager. Although the actual details vary from system to system, it won't be any different from installing any other package.

For APT-based Linux distributions (such as Debian and Ubuntu), open a terminal and type:

```
$ sudo apt-get update
$ sudo apt-get install python
```

Or if you have the **Synaptic Package Manager**, simply search for Python, mark its package for installation, and click on **Apply**.

Users of other Linux distributions are recommended to check their system documentation for information on how to use the package manager to install packages.

Installing Python on Mac OS X

Mac OS X comes pre-installed with Python. However, due to Apple's release cycle, it's often an old version. If you start the Python interactive shell and find a version older than 2.3, you should visit this URL: `http://www.python.org/download/mac/` and download the most recent installer for your version of Mac OS X.

Now that Python is up and running, we are almost ready. Next, we will install Django and make sure that we have a database system.

Installing Django

Installing Django is very easy, but the steps required for its installation depend on your operating system. Since Python is a platform-independent language, Django has one package that works everywhere regardless of your operating system.

To download Django, head to `http://www.djangoproject.com/download/`, and grab the latest official version. The code in this book was developed on Django 1.0 (the latest version at the time of writing), but most of it should run on the later official releases too. Next, follow the instructions related to your platform.

Installing Django on Windows

After you download the Django archive, extract it to the C drive and open a command prompt (by clicking on **Start**, and then **Accessories**). Change the current directory to where you extracted Django by issuing the following command, where x.xx is your Django version:

```
c:\>cd c:\Django-x.xx
```

Next, install Django by running the following command (for which you will need administrative privileges):

```
c:\Django-x.xx>python setup.py install
```

If these instructions do not work, you can manually copy the django folder in the archive to the **Lib | site-packages** folder located in the Python installation directory. This will do the job of running the setup.py install command.

 If you do not have a program to handle the .tar.gz files on your system, I recommend using 7-Zip, which is free and available at http://www.7-zip.org/.

The last step is copying the django-admin.py file from **Django-x.xx | django | bin** to somewhere in your system path, such as c:\windows or the folder where you installed Python.

Once this has been done, you can safely remove the c:\Django-x.xx folder, because it is no longer needed.

That's it. To test your installation, open a command prompt and type the following command:

```
c:\>django-admin.py --version
```

If you see the current version of Django printed on screen, then everything is set.

Installing Django on UNIX/Linux and Mac OS X

Installation instructions for all UNIX and Linux systems are the same. You need to run the following commands in the directory where the Django-x.xx.tar.gz archive is located. These commands will extract the archive and install Django for you:

```
$ tar xfz Django-x.xx.tar.gz
$ cd Django-x.xx
$ sudo python setup.py install
```

These instructions should work on any UNIX or Linux system as well as on Mac OS X. However, it may be easier to install Django through your system's package manager if it has a package for Django. Ubuntu has one, so to install Django on Ubuntu, simply look for the package python-django in Synaptic, or run the following command:

```
$ sudo apt-get install python-django
```

You can test your installation by running this command:

```
$ django-admin.py --version
```

If you are using the `python-django` package in Ubuntu, the command will be slightly different. It won't contain the `.py` extension. Keep this in mind because you will be using the `django-admin.py` again later on.

```
$ django-admin --version
```

If you see the current version of Django printed on the screen, then everything is set.

Installing a database system

While Django does not require a database to function, the application that we are going to develop does. So in the last step of software installation, we are going to make sure that we have a database system for handling our data.

It is worth noting that Django supports several database engines: MySQL, PostgreSQL, MS SQL Server, Oracle, and SQLite. Interestingly, you only need to learn one API in order to use any of these database systems. This is possibly because of Django's database layer, which abstracts access to the database system. We will learn about this later. For now you only need to know that regardless of the database system you choose, you will be able to run the Django applications developed in this book (or elsewhere) without modification.

If you have Python 2.5 or higher, you won't need to install anything as Python 2.5 comes with the SQLite database management system contained in a module named `sqlite3`. Unlike client-server database systems, SQLite does not require a resident process in memory. It stores the database in a single file, which makes it ideal for our development environment. Therefore, throughout this book, we will be using SQLite in our examples. Of course, you are free to use your preferred database management system. We can tell Django what database system to use by editing a configuration file, as we will see in later sections. It is also worth noting that if you want to use MySQL, you will need to install MySQLdb, the MySQL driver for Python.

If you don't have Python 2.5, you can manually install the python module for SQLite by downloading it from `http://www.pysqlite.org/` (for Windows users) or through your package manager (for UNIX and Linux users).

Django comes with its own web server, and we will use it during the development phase because it is lightweight and comes pre-configured for Django. However, Django does support Apache and other popular web servers such as Lighttpd. We will see how to configure Django for Apache when we prepare our application for deployment later in this book.

The same applies to the database manager. During the development phase, we will use SQLite because it is easy to set up. But when we deploy the application, we will switch to a database server such as MySQL.

As I said earlier, regardless of what components we use, our code will stay the same. Django handles all the communication with the web and database servers for us.

Creating your first project

Now that the software we need is in place, here comes the fun part—creating our first Django project!

As you may recall from the Django installation section, we used a command called `django-admin.py` to test our installation. This utility is at the heart of Django's project management facilities, as it enables the user to do a range of project management tasks. They include the following:

- Creating a new project
- Creating and managing the project's database
- Validating the current project and testing for errors
- Starting the development web server

In the rest of this chapter, we will see how to use some of these tasks and create a basis for our bookmark-sharing application in the process.

Creating an empty project

To create your first Django project, open a terminal (or command prompt for Windows users), type the following command, and hit *Enter*:

```
$ django-admin.py startproject django_bookmarks
```

This command will create a folder named `django_bookmarks` in the current directory as well as the initial directory structure inside it. Let's see what kinds of files are created:

```
django_bookmarks/
    __init__.py
    manage.py
    settings.py
    urls.py
```

Here is a quick explanation of what these files are:

File name	File description
`__init__.py`	Django projects are Python packages, and this file is required to tell Python that the folder is to be treated as a package.
	A package in Python's terminology is a collection of modules, and it is used to group similar files together and prevent naming conflicts.
`manage.py`	This is another utility script used to manage your project. You can think of it as your project's version of `django-admin.py`. Actually, both `django-admin.py` and `manage.py` share the same backend code.
`settings.py`	This is the main configuration file for your Django project. In this file you can specify a variety of options, including the database settings, site languages, the Django features are to be enabled, and so on. Various sections of this file will be explained as we build our application during the next chapters, but in this chapter we will only see how to enter the database settings.
`urls.py`	This is another configuration file. You can think of it as a mapping between URLs and Python functions that handle them. This file is one of Django's powerful features, and we will see how to utilize it in the next chapter.

When we start writing code for our application, we will create new files inside the project's folder. Thus, the folder also serves as a container for our code.

 Now that you have a general idea of the structure of a Django project, let's configure our database system.

Setting up the database

In this section, we will work with code for the first time. Therefore, we will have to choose a source code editor to enter and edit the code. There are many options in the market when it comes to source code editors. Some people prefer fully fledged IDEs, whereas others like simple text editors. The choice is totally up to you — pick whichever you feel more comfortable with. If you already use a certain program to work with Python source files, then I suggest that you stick to it, as it will work just fine with Django. Otherwise, I can make a few recommendations:

- **Scite** (also known as **Scintilla**): This editor is lightweight, yet very powerful. It is available for Linux and Windows, supports syntax highlighting and code completion, and works well with Python. It is an open source editor, and you can find it at `http://www.scintilla.org/SciTE.html`.

- **TextMate**: This popular text editor for Mac OS X also provides a rich set of features for Django developers, while being user-friendly at the same time. TextMate is not free, but there is a thirty-day trial version that you can download from `http://macromates.com/`.

- **Smultron**: This is another popular Mac OS X open source editor and has a good Python support. You can download it at `http://tuppis.com/smultron/`.

- **Eclipse + PyDev**: This combination is an integrated development environment for Python. It supports all the standard features of IDEs from source version management to integrated debugging. It takes a while to learn all of its features, but for those who prefer a complete IDE (and especially those familiar with Eclipse), it is an excellent choice. More information on installation is available at `http://pydev.sourceforge.net/`.

Now that you have a source code editor ready, let's open the `settings.py` file in the project folder and see what it contains:

```
# Django settings for django_bookmarks project.
DEBUG = True
TEMPLATE_DEBUG = DEBUG
ADMINS = (
    # ('Your Name', 'your_email@domain.com'),
)
MANAGERS = ADMINS
DATABASE_ENGINE = ''    # 'postgresql_psycopg2', 'postgresql',
                        # 'mysql', 'sqlite3' or 'ado_mssql'.
DATABASE_NAME = ''      # Or path to database file
                        # if using sqlite3.
DATABASE_USER = ''      # Not used with sqlite3.
```

```
DATABASE_PASSWORD = ''  # Not used with sqlite3.
DATABASE_HOST = ''      # Set to empty string for localhost.
                        # Not used with sqlite3.
DATABASE_PORT = ''      # Set to empty string for default.
                        # Not used with sqlite3.

# The rest of the file was trimmed.
```

As you may have already noticed, the file contains a number of variables that control various aspects of the application. Entering a new value for a variable is as simple as doing a Python assignment statement. In addition, the file is extensively commented. These comments explain what each variable controls.

What concerns us now is configuring the database. I mentioned earlier that Django supports several database systems, so first of all we have to specify the database system that we are going to use. This is controlled by the DATABASE_ENGINE variable. As we are using SQLite, set this variable to 'sqlite3'.

Next is the database name. We will choose a descriptive name for your database: Edit DATABASE_NAME and set it to 'bookmarksdb'. When using SQLite, this is all you need to do.

After those simple edits, the database section in settings.py now looks as follows:

```
DATABASE_ENGINE = 'sqlite3'
DATABASE_NAME = 'bookmarksdb'
DATABASE_USER = ''
DATABASE_PASSWORD = ''
DATABASE_HOST = ''
DATABASE_PORT = ''
```

Finally, we will tell Django to populate the configured database with tables. Although we haven't created any tables for our data yet (and we won't do so until the next chapter), Django requires several tables in the database for some of its features to function properly. Creating these tables is easy as it is only a matter of issuing the following command:

```
$ python manage.py syncdb
```

If you have entered this command and everything is correct, status messages will scroll on the screen indicating that the tables are being created. When prompted for the superuser account, enter your preferred username, email address, and password. It is important to create a superuser account, without which you won't be able to gain access to your initial web page once you have created it. If, on the other hand, the database is misconfigured, an error message will be printed to help you troubleshoot the issue. The command will create a file known as bookmarksdb in your project directory. This file will contain your application's data.

With this done, we are ready to launch our application.

Using `python manage.py`:
When running a command that starts with `python manage.py`, make sure that you are currently in the project's directory where `manage.py` is located.

Launching the development server

As discussed earlier, Django comes with a lightweight web server for developing and testing applications. This server is pre-configured to work with Django, and more importantly, it restarts whenever you modify the code.

To start the server, run the following command:

```
$ python manage.py runserver
```

Next, open your browser, and navigate to `http://localhost:8000/`. You should see a welcome message as shown in the following screenshot:

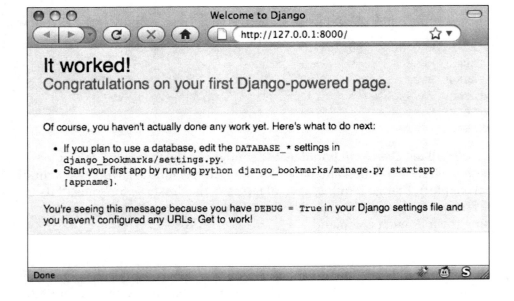

As you may have noticed, the web server runs on port 8000 by default. If you want to change the port, you can specify it in the command line:

```
$ python manage.py runserver <port number>
```

Congratulations! You have created and configured your first Django project. This project will be the basis on which we will build our bookmarking application. In the next chapter, we will start developing our application. The page displayed by the web server will be replaced by something that we will have written ourselves!

Summary

In this chapter, we prepared our development environment, created our first project, and learned how to launch the Django development server. We are now ready to start building our social bookmarking application.

Here is a quick summary of the Django features covered in this chapter:

- Django can be downloaded from the official Django website at http://www.djangoproject.com/. Given that it is written in Python, the same package works on all major operating systems.

- To start a new Django project, issue the following command:

  ```
  $ django-admin.py startproject <project-name>
  ```

- To create database tables, issue the following command:

  ```
  $ python manage.py syncdb
  ```

- To start the development server, issue the following command:

  ```
  $ python manage.py runserver
  ```

- Django project settings are stored in the settings.py file. This file is a regular Python source file that can be edited using any source code editor. To change a variable, simply assign the desired value to it.

The next chapter takes you through a tour of the main Django components and develops a working prototype for our bookmark sharing application. It's going to be a fun chapter with many new things to learn. So, keep reading!

3
Building a Social Bookmarking Application

In the previous chapter we learned how to create an empty project, enter the database settings, and run the development server. Now, we will start writing our bookmark-sharing application and learn about views, models, and templates in the process.

You can think of this chapter as a prolonged tour of the main Django components. You will learn how to create dynamic pages using views, store and manage data in the database using models, and simplify page generation using templates. While learning about these features, you will form a solid idea of how Django components work and interact with each other. The later chapters will explore these components deeper, as we develop more features and add them to our application.

The following topics are covered in this chapter:

- URLs and views: Creating the main page
- Models: Designing an initial database schema
- Templates: Creating a template for the main page
- Putting it all together: Generating user pages

A word about Django terminology

Django is an MVC framework. However, the controller is called the "view", and the view is called the "template". The view in Django is the component which retrieves and manipulates data, whereas the template is the component that presents data to the user. For this reason, Django is sometimes known as an **MTV** framework (where MTV stands for **model, template**, and **view**). This different terminology neither changes the fact that Django is an MVC framework, nor affects how applications are developed. But keep the terminology in mind to avoid possible confusion if you have worked with other MVC frameworks in the past.

URLs and views: creating the main page

The first thing that comes to mind after seeing the welcome page of the development server is: How can we change it? To create our own welcome page, we need to define an entry point to our application in the form of a URL and tell Django to call a particular Python function when a visitor accesses this URL. We will write this Python function ourselves, and make it display our own welcome message.

Creating the main page view

A **view** in Django terminology is a regular Python function that responds to a page request by generating the corresponding page. To write our first Django view for the main page, we first need to create a Django **application** inside our project. You can think of an application as a container for views and data models. To create it, issue the following command within our django_bookmarks folder:

```
$ python manage.py startapp bookmarks
```

The syntax of application creation is very similar to that of project creation. We used startapp as the first parameter to python manage.py, and provided bookmarks as the name of our application.

After running this command, Django will create a folder named bookmarks inside the project folder with these three files:

- __init__.py: This file tells Python that bookmarks is a Python package
- views.py: This file will contain our views
- models.py: This file will contain our data models

Now, let's create the main page view. Open the file bookmarks/views.py in your code editor and enter the following:

```python
from django.http import HttpResponse
def main_page(request):
  output = u'''
    <html>
      <head><title>%s</title></head>
      <body>
        <h1>%s</h1><p>%s</p>
      </body>
    </html>
  ''' % (
    u'Django Bookmarks',
    u'Welcome to Django Bookmarks',
    u'Where you can store and share bookmarks!'
  )
  return HttpResponse(output)
```

The code is short and pretty straightforward. Let's go through it line by line:

- We import the class `HttpResponse` from `django.http`. We need this class in order to generate our response page.

- We define a Python function that takes one parameter named `request`. This parameter contains user input and other information. For example, `request.GET`, `request.POST`, and `request.COOKIES` are dictionaries that contain get, post, and cookie data respectively.

- We build the HTML code of the response page, wrap it within an `HttpResponse` object, and return it. Django uses Unicode to store and present data. Because of this, we added the letter u before strings to make them Unicode strings. This is how a Unicode string is created in Python. Throughout this book, we will use Unicode for all strings that are presented in the web pages or stored in the database. This means that whenever a string will be a part of a webpage or will be saved in the database, the letter u would need to be added before it.

A Django view is just a regular Python function. It takes user input as a parameter, and returns page output. But before we can see the output of this view, we need to connect it to a URL.

Embedding HTML snippets within views is usually not recommended for a variety of reasons. We did it here for the sake of simplicity. Later in this chapter, we will learn how to put the HTML code of our site in a separate set of files.

Creating the main page URL

As you may recall from the previous chapter, a file named `urls.py` was created when we started our project. This file contains valid URLs for our application, and maps each URL to a view that is a Python function. Let's examine the contents of this file and see how to edit it:

```
from django.conf.urls.defaults import *
urlpatterns = patterns('',
    # Example:
    # (r'^django_bookmarks/',
        include('django_bookmarks.foo.urls')),
    # Uncomment this for admin:
    # (r'^admin/', include('django.contrib.admin.urls')),
)
```

As you can probably tell, the file contains a table of URLs and their corresponding Python functions (or views). The table is called `urlpatterns`, and it initially contains example entries that are commented out. Each entry is a Python tuple that consists of a URL and its view.

The URL syntax may look familiar to you because it uses regular expressions. Django gives you a lot of flexibility by letting you specify URL patterns with the use of this powerful string-matching technique. We will gradually learn about this syntax and how to utilize it. Let's start by removing the comments and adding an entry for the main page:

```
from django.conf.urls.defaults import *
from bookmarks.views import *

urlpatterns = patterns('',
    (r'^$', main_page),
)
```

Again, let's see the breakdown of this code:

- The file imports everything from the module `django.conf.urls.defaults`. This module provides the necessary functions to define URLs.
- We import everything from `bookmarks.views`. This is necessary to access our views and connect them to URLs.
- The `patterns` function is used to define the URL table. It contains only one mapping for now—from `r'^$'` to our view `main_page`.

One last thing needs to be explained before we see the view in action. The regular expression that we used will look a bit strange if you haven't used regular expressions before. It is a raw string that contains two characters, `^` and `$`. The Python syntax for defining **raw** strings is `r''`. If Python encounters such a raw string, backslashes and other escape sequences are retained in the string rather than interpreted in any way. In this syntax, backslashes are left in the string without change, and escape sequences are not interpreted. This is useful when working with regular expressions because they often contain backslashes.

In regular expressions, `^` means the beginning of the string, and `$` means the end of the string. So `^$` is basically a string that doesn't contain anything, meaning it is an empty string. Given that we are writing the view of the main page, the URL of the page is the root URL, and indeed it should be empty.

Python documentation of the `re` module covers regular expressions in detail. I recommend reading it if you want a thorough treatment of regular expressions. You can find the documentation online at:

```
http://docs.python.org/lib/module-re.html
```

The following table summarizes regular expression syntax for those who want a quick refresher:

Symbol / Expression	Matched string
. (Dot)	Any character
^ (Caret)	Start of string
$	End of string
*	0 or more repetitions
+	1 or more repetitions
?	0 or 1 repetitions
		A	B means A or B
[a-z]	Any lowercase character
\w	Any alphanumeric character or _
\d	Any digit

Now that everything is clear, we can test our first view. Launch the development server and go to `http://127.0.0.1:8000/` to see the page generated by the view.

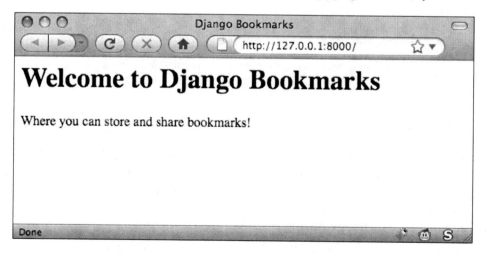

Congratulations! Your first Django view is up and running.

Before we move to the next section, it is a good idea to understand what's going on behind the scenes:

- When a user requests the root URL at `http://127.0.0.1:8000/`, Django searches the URL table in the `urls.py` file for a URL that matches the request. Matching is done using regular expressions.

- If Django finds a matching URL, it calls its corresponding view. The view, which is a regular Python function, receives data generated by the user's browser as a parameter called the `request` object. It returns the generated page wrapped in an `HttpResponse` object.

- If Django doesn't find a URL that matches the request, it displays a **Page not found (404)** error. You can test this by requesting `http://127.0.0.1:8000/ does_not_exist/` as illustrated in the following image. Notice that Django displays helpful debugging information to assist you in figuring out what's wrong. Of course, these debugging messages can be turned off when the site goes live.

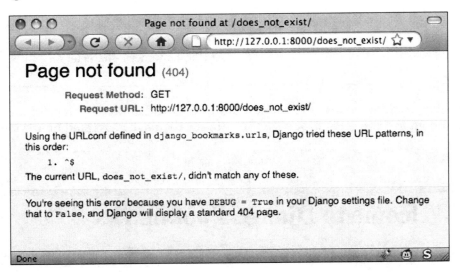

This way of mapping URLs to views gives the developer a lot of flexibility. URLs are not restricted to filenames as in PHP, and are not automatically mapped to function names as in `mod_python`. You are given total control over the mapping between URLs and functions. This is especially good for large projects, where URLs and function names often change during phases of the development.

Our main page looks a little basic without CSS. Therefore, we will learn to use templates, which will make it easy to style our pages using stylesheets. Before doing this, we will learn about database models as well as how to store and manage our data.

Models: designing an initial database schema

Almost every Web 2.0 application requires a database to store and manage its data. The database engine is a fundamental component of web development today. Web applications offer the user a UI to enter and manage his or her data, and use a database engine behind the scenes to manage this data.

 In Django, you can think of view as the component responsible for collecting and displaying data, and the model as the component responsible for storing and managing it.

We will choose the database engine that configured our database settings in the previous chapter. In this section, we will make use of the database to store and manage user accounts and bookmarks.

If you are used to dealing with the database directly through SQL queries, then you may find Django's approach to database access a bit different. Loosely speaking, Django abstracts access to database tables through Python classes. To store, manipulate, and retrieve objects from the database, the developer uses a Python-based API. To do this, SQL knowledge is useful but not required.

This technique is best explained with an example. For our bookmarking application, we need to store three types of data in the database:

- Users (ID, username, password, email)
- Links (ID, URL)
- Bookmarks (ID, title, user_id, link_id)

Each user will have his or her own entry in the Users table. This entry stores the username, password, and email ID. Similarly, each link will have a corresponding entry in the links table. We will only store the link's URL for now.

As for the Bookmarks table, you can think of it as the joining table between Users and Links. When a user adds a bookmark, an entry for the bookmark's URL is added to the links table (if it doesn't already exist), and then a joining entry is added to the Bookmarks table. This entry connects the user with the link, and stores the title that the user entered for the bookmark.

To convert this table design into a Python code, we need to edit the `models.py` file in `bookmarks` and enter the details of each object type. The `models.py` file is the file where database models are stored, and contains only an `import` line when it's created by `manage.py startapp`.

The link data model

Let's start by creating the data model for the Links table because it's the simplest one. Open the `bookmarks/models.py` file in your editor and type the following code:

```
from django.db import models

class Link(models.Model):
    url = models.URLField(unique=True)
```

Going through the code line by line, we learn the following:

- The `models` package contains classes that are required to define models, so it is imported first.
- We define a class named `Link`. This class inherits from `models.Model`, which is the base class for all models. The class contains one field named `url`, and it's of the type `models.URLField`. This field must be unique.

The `models.URLField` is one of the many field types provided by Django. The following is a partial table of these field types:

Field type	Description
IntegerField	An integer
TextField	A large text field
DateTimeField	A date and time field
EmailField	An email field with 75 characters max.
URLField	A URL field with 200 characters max.
FileField	A file-upload field

You can find a complete list of the available field types in the online documentation at:

http://docs.djangoproject.com/en/dev/ref/models/fields/.

To use the Link model, we first need to activate it in our Django project. This is done by editing the `settings.py` file, looking for the `INSTALLED_APPS` variable, and adding our application name (`django_bookmarks.bookmarks`) to it:

```
INSTALLED_APPS = (
    'django.contrib.auth',
    'django.contrib.contenttypes',
    'django.contrib.sessions',
    'django.contrib.sites',
    'django_bookmarks.bookmarks',
)
```

Now, issue the following command to create a table for the Link data model in the database:

```
$ python manage.py syncdb
```

You may remember that we used this command in the previous chapter to create Django's own administrative tables. Whenever you add a data model, you need to issue this command in order to create its table in the database.

If you are familiar with SQL, you can examine the SQL query generated by Django by running the following command:

```
$ python manage.py sql bookmarks
```

The output from this command may differ slightly depending on your database engine. For SQLite, it should look similar to this:

```
BEGIN;
CREATE TABLE "bookmarks_link" (
    "id" integer NOT NULL PRIMARY KEY,
    "url" varchar(200) NOT NULL UNIQUE
);
COMMIT;
```

What has happened here? Django analyzed our Link model, which is a regular Python class, and generated an SQL CREATE statement for a database table named bookmarks_link. This table will store instances of the Link class. Notice that Django automatically added an id field to the table. This field is the primary key of the table and can be used to identify links and connect them to bookmarks.

The power of Django's Python database API does not stop at creating tables. We can use it to create entries in the table, modify entries, search and browse the table contents, and much more. To explore the API, we will use the Python interactive console. To launch the console, use the following command:

```
$ python manage.py shell
```

This shell differs from the standard Python shell in two ways. First, the project path is added to sys.path. This simplifies the import of modules from our project. Second, a special environment variable is created to hold the path to our settings.py file. So, whenever you need a Python shell to interact with your project, use the above command.

Now import the contents of the models module:

```
>>> from bookmarks.models import *
```

To add a new link, create a new instance of the `Link` class and call the `save` method on it:

```
>>> link1 = Link(url=u'http://www.packtpub.com/')
>>> link1.save()
>>> link2 = Link(url=u'http://www.example.com/')
>>> link2.save()
```

We call the `save` method to store the object in the database. Before that, the object exists in memory only, and will be lost if you close the console. However, when you call `save`, the object is stored in the database.

Table fields become attributes of objects. To examine and change a link's URL, type the following:

```
>>> link2.url
        u'http://www.example.com/'
>>> link2.url = u'http://www.google.com/'
>>> link2.save()
```

To get a list of all available `Link` objects, type the following:

```
>>> links = Link.objects.all()
>>> for link in links:
...     print link.url
...
http://www.packtpub.com/
http://www.google.com/
```

To get an object by ID, type the following:

```
>>> Link.objects.get(id=1)
        <Link: Link object>
```

Finally, to delete a link, use the following:

```
>>> link2.delete()
>>> Link.objects.count()
        1
```

An output of 1 indicates that there is now only one remaining link. Notice that we were able to do all of this without needing a single SQL statement. Django's model API can do a lot more—it covers all the tasks commonly done through SQL.

Actually, the above method calls are converted to SQL statements, and the results of the statements are returned. The benefits of this approach are numerous, some of which are as follows:

- You don't have to learn another language to access the database. You already know Python and how to use it to write views, so it's obviously a benefit if you can also use it to access the database.
- Django transparently handles the conversion between Python objects and table rows. You only work with Python objects, and Django automatically stores and retrieves them from the database for you.
- You don't have to worry about any special SQL syntax for different database engines, especially if you have to switch from one engine to another. The Django model API is the same no matter what engine you use, and it takes care of the differences for you.

The user data model

Now that you are comfortable with the concept of data models, let's move to the User object. Fortunately for us, management of user accounts is so common that Django comes with a user model ready for us to use. This model contains fields that are often associated with user accounts, such as username, password and email, and so on. The model is called User and is located in the `django.contrib.auth.models` package.

To explore the contents of this model, open the interactive console and type the following:

```
>>> from django.contrib.auth.models import User
>>> User.objects.all()
        [<User: ayman>]
```

We can see that the table represented by this model already contains a user. Remember how we configured the database in the previous chapter? We had to create the superuser account and Django stored this user in the table of the User model.

You can use the `dir` function to examine the fields of User objects:

```
>>> user = User.objects.get(id=1)
>>> dir(user)
```

You will get a very long list of attributes. Among them you will find the username, email address, and password. Good news! This model fulfills our needs. Django provides all the necessary attributes for our user objects, so we can directly use the User model without any extra code.

The bookmark data model

Only one model remains—the `Bookmark` model. When we examined it earlier, we realized that a bookmark connects a user to a link. A bookmark belongs to one user and one link. However, one user may have many bookmarks, and one link may be bookmarked by many users. In the database terminology we say there is a many-to-many relationship between users and links. However, there is no way to actually represent a many-to-many relationship such as this one using a standard database system. In our particular case, we will invent the concept of a bookmark to break up this many-to-many relationship into its constituent one-to-many relationships.

The first of these is the one-to-many relationship between the user and their bookmarks. One user can have many bookmarks, but each bookmark is associated with only one user. That is to say, each user can bookmark a particular link once.

The second of these is the one-to-many relationship between a link and its bookmarks. One link can have many bookmarks associated with it if multiple users have bookmarked it, but each bookmark is associated with only one link.

Now that we have two separate one-to-many relationships, it is possible to represent all of this in a database system. To do so, we create a third table—the bookmarks table—that connects the user table and the links table. Each row in the bookmarks table has a reference to a row in the users table (that is, to a particular user) and a reference to the links table (that is, to a particular link). In SQL, these references to rows in "foreign" tables are known as foreign keys. But instead of working with SQL to define tables and foreign keys, we will use the Django model's API to write a data model for the bookmarks.

The following code listing contains the Bookmark data model. You should insert it into the `bookmarks/models.py` file. For those who are new to relational databases and SQL, this section may seem a little obscure at first. However, it will all make more sense when you see it in action. Here is the code for the Bookmark data model:

```
from django.contrib.auth.models import User
class Bookmark(models.Model):
    title = models.CharField(max_length=200)
    user = models.ForeignKey(User)
    link = models.ForeignKey(Link)
```

We first import the `User` class in order to refer to it in the Bookmark model. Next, we define a class for the Bookmark model as we did with `Link`. The new model contains a text field called `title`, and two foreign keys that refer back to the `User` and `Link` models.

Code snippets and import statements

Python conventions suggest putting `import` statements at the beginning of the source file. When adding code to an existing file, new `import` statements will be present at the beginning of the new code snippet, but I recommend you to move these statements to the beginning of the file.

After you enter the model's code into the `models.py` file, you need to run `manage.py syncdb` to create its corresponding table.

Let's examine the SQL query generated by Django to see how it automatically handles foreign keys. Again, issue the following command:

$ python manage.py sql bookmarks

And you will see the CREATE statement for the `Bookmark` data model:

```
BEGIN;
CREATE TABLE "bookmarks_link" (
    "id" integer NOT NULL PRIMARY KEY,
    "url" varchar(200) NOT NULL UNIQUE
);
CREATE TABLE "bookmarks_bookmark" (
    "id" integer NOT NULL PRIMARY KEY,
    "title" varchar(200) NOT NULL,
    "user_id" integer NOT NULL
      REFERENCES "auth_user" ("id"),
    "link_id" integer NOT NULL
      REFERENCES "bookmarks_link" ("id")
);
COMMIT;
```

Notice how Django appended `_id` to the table name to create foreign key fields and generated the necessary SQL query for expressing one-to-many relationships.

Now that the data models are ready, we have the facilities to store and manage our data. Django offers an elegant and straightforward Python API to store Python objects in the database. It thus spares the developer the burden of working with SQL and converting between SQL and Python types and idioms.

Next, we will learn about another major Django component: the template system. We will use it to simplify our working with page creation, and then make use of all the information we learned in this chapter to create bookmark-listing pages for users.

Templates: creating a template for the main page

In the first section of this chapter, we created a very simple view for our application's main page. We had to embed the HTML code of the page into the view's code. This approach has many disadvantages even for a basic view:

- Good software engineering practices always emphasize the separation between UI and logic, because it enhances reusability. On the other hand, embedding HTML within the Python code clearly violates this rule.

- Editing HTML embedded within Python requires Python knowledge. But this is impractical for many development teams whose web designers do not know Python.

- Handling HTML code within the Python code is a tedious and error-prone task. For example, quotation marks in HTML may need to be escaped in Python strings, and the overall result may be unclean and unreadable code.

Therefore, we'd better separate Django views from HTML code generation before continuing with our application. Fortunately for us, Django provides a component that facilitates this task. It is called the template system.

The idea of this system is simple. Instead of embedding HTML code in the view, you store it in a separate file known as a template. This template may contain placeholders for dynamic sections that are generated in the view. When generating a page, the view loads the template and passes dynamic values to it. In turn, the template replaces the placeholders with these values and generates the page.

To help you better understand the concept, let's apply it to our `main_page` view. First of all, to keep our directory structure clean, we will create a separate folder called `templates` in our project folder. Next, we need to inform Django of our newly-created `templates` folder. So, open the `settings.py` file, look for the `TEMPLATE_DIRS` variable, and add the absolute path of your templates folder to it. If you don't want to hardcode the path into `settings.py` file, you can use the following little snippet that will also work:

```
import os.path

TEMPLATE_DIRS = (
    os.path.join(os.path.dirname(__file__), 'templates'),
)
```

Next, create a file called `main_page.html` in the templates folder with the following content:

```
<html>
  <head>
    <title>{{ head_title }}</title>
  </head>
  <body>
    <h1>{{ page_title }}</h1>
    <p>{{ page_body }}</p>
  </body>
</html>
```

The structure of the template is very similar to the HTML code that we embedded in the `main_page` view. However, there is one small difference. We used a special syntax to indicate sections that we wanted to change in the view. For example, {{ head_title }} indicates a variable called `head_title` that can be changed inside the view. Template variables are always surrounded by double braces.

Now, let's see how to use this template in the view. Edit the `bookmarks/views.py` file and replace its contents with the following code:

```
from django.http import HttpResponse
from django.template import Context
from django.template.loader import import get_template

def main_page(request):
  template = get_template('main_page.html')
  variables = Context({
    'head_title': u'Django Bookmarks',
    'page_title': u'Welcome to Django Bookmarks',
    'page_body': u'Where you can store and share bookmarks!'
  })
  output = template.render(variables)
  return HttpResponse(output)
```

As usual, we will go through the code line by line:

- To load a template, we used the `get_template` method, which is found in the `django.template.loader` module. This method takes the filename of a template and returns a template object.

- To set variable values in the template, we created an object called `variables` of type `Context`. The constructor for this type takes a Python dictionary whose keys are variable names (without double braces), and whose values are the values of these variables.

- To replace template variables and create HTML output from the template, we used the `render` method. This method takes a `Context` object as a parameter, so here we pass the `variables` object to it.

- Finally, we returned the HTML output wrapped in an `HttpResponse` object.

As you can see, the benefits of this approach over the old one are clear. We no longer have to deal with HTML within Python. Putting the HTML code into its own file is a lot cleaner. In addition, the template system provided by Django makes template management an easy and straightforward task.

The template system offers a lot in addition to a variable substitution. It provides conditional statements to test whether a variable is empty or not, and a `for` loop to iterate through a list and print its items, and so on. We will see how to employ some of these features in the next section, in which we will use all the knowledge that we have gained previously to create user pages.

Putting it all together: generating user pages

This chapter has covered a lot of material. It has introduced the concepts of views, models, and templates. In the final section, we will write another view and make use of all the information that we have learned so far. This view will display a list of all the bookmarks that belong to a certain user.

Creating the URL

The URL of this view will have the form `user/username`, where *username* is the owner of the bookmarks that we want to see. This URL is different from the first URL that we added because it contains a dynamic portion. So we will have to employ the power of regular expressions in order to express this URL. Open the `urls.py` file and edit it so that the URL table looks like this:

```
urlpatterns = patterns('',
  (r'^$', main_page),
  (r'^user/(\w+)/$', user_page),
)
```

The pattern here looks more complicated than the first one. \w means an alphanumeric character or an underscore. The + sign after it causes the regular expression to match one or more repetitions of what precedes the sign. So, in effect, \w+ means any string that consists of alphanumeric characters and possibly the underscore. We have surrounded this portion of the regular expression with parentheses. This will cause Django to capture the string that matches this portion, and pass it to the view. For example, if the requested URL is `user/test/`, `test` will match `\w+` since it consists of alphanumeric characters. Django will call the `user_page` view as a result, and pass the string `'test'` to it. We will see this in action in the next section.

Writing the view

Now that we've added an entry for the new URL to the URL table, let's write the actual view for it. Open the `bookmarks/views.py` file and enter the following code:

```
from django.http import HttpResponse, Http404
from django.contrib.auth.models import User

def user_page(request, username):
  try:
    user = User.objects.get(username=username)
  except User.DoesNotExist:
    raise Http404(u'Requested user not found.')
  bookmarks = user.bookmark_set.all()
  template = get_template('user_page.html')
  variables = Context({
    'username': username,
    'bookmarks': bookmarks
  })
  output = template.render(variables)
  return HttpResponse(output)
```

Most of the view should already look familiar. Therefore, we will only examine what's new:

- Unlike our first view, `user_page` takes an extra parameter in addition to the familiar request object. Remember that the pattern for this URL contains capturing parentheses. The strings captured by URL patterns are passed as parameters to views. The captured string in this URL is passed as the `username` parameter.

- We used `User.objects.get` to obtain the user object whose username is requested. We can use a similar technique to query any table by a unique column. This method throws an exception named `DoesNotExist` if there are no records that match the query.

- If the requested username is not available in the database, we generate a **Page not found (404)** error by raising an exception of the type `Http404`.

- To obtain the list of bookmarks for a particular user object, we can conveniently use the `bookmark_set` attribute available in the user object. Django detects relationships between data models and automatically generates such attributes. There is no need to worry about constructing SQL `JOIN` queries ourselves to obtain user bookmarks, for example.

Designing the template

The previous view loads a template called `user_page.html` and passes the username and bookmarks to it. We will write this template now. Create a file called `user_page.html` in the `templates` directory and enter the following code into it:

```
<html>
  <head>
    <title>Django Bookmarks - User: {{ username }}</title>
  </head>
  <body>
    <h1>Bookmarks for {{ username }}</h1>
    {% if bookmarks %}
      <ul>
        {% for bookmark in bookmarks %}
          <li><a href="{{ bookmark.link.url }}">
            {{ bookmark.title }}</a></li>
        {% endfor %}
      </ul>
    {% else %}
      <p>No bookmarks found.</p>
    {% endif %}
  </body>
</html>
```

This template is more involved than our first one. In addition to variables, it uses an `if` condition and a `for` loop to display bookmarks. The `bookmarks` variable is a list object, so we can't output it directly in the template. We have to make sure that it's not empty, and then iterate through its items.

We can check whether a variable in a template is empty or not by using the following syntax:

```
{% if variable %}
  <p>variable contains data.</p>
{% else %}
  <p>variable is empty</p>
{% endif %}
```

This `if` condition works as expected. If the variable contains data, only the first line is printed to the browser. On the other hand, if the variable is indeed empty, only the second line is printed.

To iterate through a list and print its items, we use the following syntax:

```
{% for item in list %}
  {{ item }}
{% endfor %}
```

Finally, if a variable has attributes, you can access them in a way similar to Python:

```
{{ variable.attribute }}
```

We utilized the constructs above to create the `user_page.html` template. First, it checks whether `bookmarks` is empty or not. If `bookmarks` contains items, a `for` loop iterates through them and creates links from them. If `bookmarks` is empty, a message is printed saying so.

Now, launch the development server and direct your browser to `http://127.0.0.1:8000/user/your_username/` (replacing *your_username* with your actual username). You should see something similar to the following screenshot:

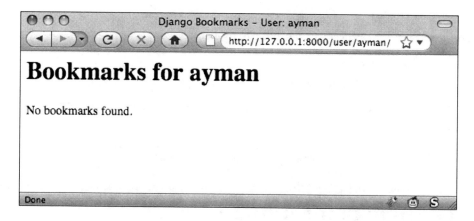

Our template worked, but the list of bookmarks is empty. This is a good opportunity to experiment with the data model API and add some bookmarks through the interactive console. As we saw earlier, you can start the console by running the following command:

```
$ python manage.py shell
```

Populating the model with data

First, obtain references to your user object and the link we created in the data models section:

```
>>> from django.contrib.auth.models import User
>>> from bookmarks.models import *
>>> user = User.objects.get(id=1)
>>> link = Link.objects.get(id=1)
```

Notice that `user.bookmark_set` is empty.

```
>>> user.bookmark_set.all()
      []
```

Now create an object that connects the two.

```
>>> bookmark = Bookmark(
...     title=u'Packt Publishing',
...     user=user,
...     link=link
... )
>>> bookmark.save()
```

Examine the `user.bookmark_set` attribute again.

```
>>> user.bookmark_set.all()
      [<Bookmark: Bookmark object>]
```

Great! Our user object now has a bookmark. Refresh the page in your browser to see the change.

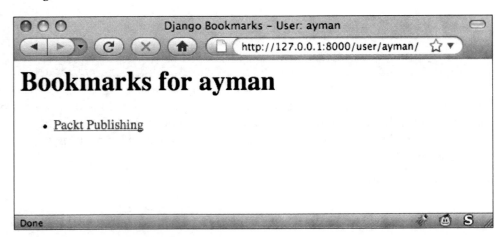

Experiment with adding more bookmarks if you like. You can access a bookmark's owner by using `bookmark.user`. This is another attribute that is automatically generated by Django. Because the relationship between users and bookmarks is one-to-many, each user has a set of bookmarks accessible through the `user.bookmark_set` attribute, whereas each bookmark has exactly one owner who is accessible through the `bookmark.user` attribute.

Summary

In this chapter, we learned about the three main components of Django: the view, model, and template. We wrote data models to store the data of our application, and then created views and templates to display this data. We also learned how to map URLs to views, and how to use the interactive console to experiment with our Django project.

The following is a summary of the Django features covered in this chapter:

- To create an application within a project, run the following command:

  ```
  $ python manage.py startapp <app-name>
  ```

- After writing a data model, the following command should be run to create the corresponding tables in the database:

  ```
  $ python manage.py syncdb
  ```

- To view the SQL queries generated by Django, issue the following command:

  ```
  $ python manage.py sql <app-name>
  ```

- Data models provide a variety of methods to interact with the database engine:
  - The `save` method saves an object into the database
  - The `objects.get` method retrieves an object by a unique field
  - The `objects.all` method retrieves a list of all objects
  - The `delete` method deletes an object from the database

- To generate a **Page not found (404)** error, raise an exception of type `Http404`.

In the next chapter, we will continue developing our application, but we will focus mostly on user management features, such as registration and logging in. The next chapter provides a lot of useful information, so read on!

4
User Registration and Management

User registration and account management are universal features found in every web application. Users need to identify themselves to the application before they can post and share content with other users. User accounts are also required for activities such as online discussions and friend networks. Therefore, this chapter will focus on building features related to account registration and management, and on taking advantage of the user authentication system that comes with Django.

In this chapter, you will learn how to:

- Create a login page
- Enable logout functionality
- Create a registration form
- Enable users to update their account information

While developing these, we will learn about two important Django features:

- Template inheritance
- The forms library

Session authentication

In the previous chapter, we learned about the user data model and used it to store user information in the database. In fact, this data model is a part of a larger Django application that provides a variety of features related to user authentication and management. The Django authentication system is available in the `django.contrib.auth` package. It is installed by default as part of Django and projects created with the `django-admin.py` utility have it enabled by default.

You can double-check to make sure that you have the authentication system enabled by examining the `INSTALLED_APPS` variable in `settings.py`. This variable contains the names of the applications available for your project. You may remember that we had to edit this variable and add the `bookmarks` application that we created ourselves. The variable should look similar to the following:

```
INSTALLED_APPS = (
  'django.contrib.auth',
  'django.contrib.contenttypes',
  'django.contrib.sessions',
  'django.contrib.sites',
  'django_bookmarks.bookmarks',
)
```

In the future, whenever you need to activate an application for your project, you can simply add its package name to the `INSTALLED_APPS` variable. Depending on the application, you may also need to run `python manage.py syncdb` to create the application's data models in the database. After that, the application will become available in your project.

Before we start using the authentication system, let's have a quick look at the features that it provides:

- **Users**: A comprehensive user data model with fields commonly required by web applications
- **Permissions**: Yes/No flags that indicate whether a user may access a certain feature or not
- **Groups**: A data model for grouping more than one user together and applying the same set of permissions to them
- **Messages**: Provides the functionality for displaying information and error messages to the user

We will only use features related to user management in this chapter. Later chapters will explore other features in detail.

Creating the login page

When we examined the user data model in the previous chapter, we noticed that it already contained a user account. This account was created during the process of starting a new project. So the natural question to ask is: "How do we log into this account?"

Those who have worked on programming a session management system in a low-level web framework (such as PHP and its library) will know that this task is not straightforward. There are many things that could go wrong in such a task, and a little mistake may open the system to security problems. Fortunately, Django developers have carefully implemented a session management system for us and activating it only requires exposing certain views to the user. We don't have to worry about managing user sessions or checking passwords. All of these are already implemented and are ready to be used.

To introduce the session system into our project, let's start with the login page. First of all, you need to add a new URL entry to the `urls.py` file. Open the file in your editor and change it so that the URL table looks like the following snippet:

```
urlpatterns = patterns('',
  (r'^$', main_page),
  (r'^user/(\w+)/$', user_page),
  (r'^login/$', 'django.contrib.auth.views.login'),
)
```

The new URL entry is slightly different from the previous ones. Instead of providing the view, we are passing its module path as a string. This is a convenient shortcut from Django, and it is often used with views that come from a package outside the current project. Django will automatically import the view for us. The path starts with `django.contrib`, which is a package that contains various add-ons for Django. As you can tell, the authentication system lives in this package.

The module `django.contrib.auth.views` contains a number of views related to session management. We have only exposed the login view for now. As its name suggests, this view handles user login requests. But before we can see it in action, we need to write a template for it.

The `login` view requires the availability of a template called `registration/login.html` in the `templates` directory. It loads this template and passes an object that represents the login form to it. We will learn about form objects in detail when we create a user registration form. But for now, we only need to know that this object is called `form` and has the following attributes: `form.username`, `form.password` and `form.has_errors`. When printed, the first two attributes generate HTML code for the username and password text fields, whereas `form.has_errors` is a Boolean attribute that is set to true if logging in fails after submitting the form.

The next step is creating a template for the view. Make a directory named `registration` within the `templates` directory, and create a file called `login.html` in it. Enter the following code into `registration/login.html`:

```
<html>
  <head>
    <title>Django Bookmarks - User Login</title>
  </head>
```

```
<body>
  <h1>User Login</h1>
  {% if form.errors %}
    <p>Your username and password didn't match.
      Please try again.</p>
  {% endif %}
  <form method="post" action=".">
    <p><label for="id_username">Username:</label>
      {{ form.username }}</p>
    <p><label for="id_password">Password:</label>
      {{ form.password }}</p>
    <input type="hidden" name="next" value="/" />
    <input type="submit" value="login" />
  </form>
</body>
</html>
```

The code in this template should look familiar by now. We first check to see if there is a login error from a previous login attempt. Then we create an HTML form that contains username and password fields, as well as a submit button and a hidden field called `next`. This hidden variable contains a URL that tells the view where to redirect the user after he or she has successfully logged in. We will redirect the user to the main page for now. The action attribute of the form is set to `"."`, which means that the form will send its data to the URL it originated from when it is submitted.

We are ready to try the login view! Run the development server and navigate to `http://127.0.0.1:8000/login/`. You will be greeted by the following login page:

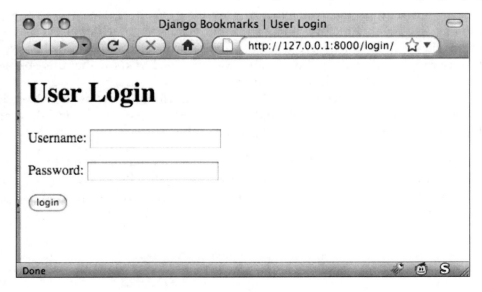

Remember when you created the database in Chapter 2? You had to enter a username and password for the superuser account after running `python manage.py syncdb`. You can use this account to log in. So either go ahead and enter your credentials or try a wrong password to see the error message. After successfully logging in, you will be redirected to the main page.

Now that we can log in, it is a good idea to make the main page indicate whether you are logged in or not. So let's rewrite its view and template. First open the `templates/main_page.html` file and replace its contents with the following:

```
<html>
  <head>
    <title>Django Bookmarks</title>
  </head>
  <body>
    <h1>Welcome to Django Bookmarks</h1>
    {% if user.username %}
      <p>Welcome {{ user.username }}!
        Here you can store and share bookmarks!</p>
    {% else %}
      <p>Welcome anonymous user!
      You need to <a href="/login/">login</a>
      before you can store and share bookmarks.</p>
    {% endif %}
  </body>
</html>
```

The template now checks whether a variable called `user.username` is set or not. If it is, the logged-in user is greeted; otherwise, a link to the login page is displayed. The template assumes that the `user` variable is passed to it. (The user variable is a Django object that we will learn about shortly.) So let's modify the main page view to reflect this. Open `bookmarks/views.py` and change the view as follows:

```
def main_page(request):
    template = get_template('main_page.html')
    variables = Context({'user': request.user})
    output = template.render(variables)
    return HttpResponse(output)
```

The code simply loads the main page template, passes `request.user` (which contains the current user object) to it, and renders the page. You can access the current user object at `request.user`. (We will learn about this very soon.)

Reload the main page and you will see a friendlier message that mentions the logged in username, as in the following screenshot:

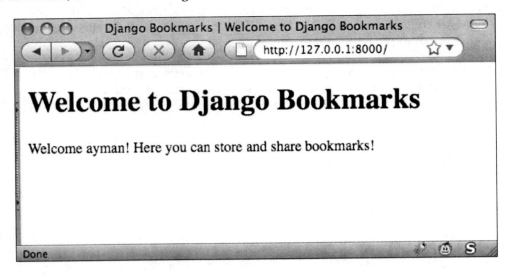

You may have noticed by now that loading a template, passing variables to it, and rendering the page is a very common task. Indeed, it is so common that Django provides a shortcut for it. Once again, let's rewrite the main page view in bookmarks/views.py to make use of this shortcut:

```
from django.shortcuts import render_to_response
def main_page(request):
  return render_to_response(
    'main_page.html',
    {'user': request.user}
  )
```

Using the render_to_response method from the django.shortcuts package, we have reduced the view to one statement. This method takes the template name and a dictionary of template variables as parameters, and returns an HttpResponse object.

The user object available at request.user is the same type of User object as we have dealt with before. We are already familiar with its data fields, so let's learn about some of its methods:

- is_authenticated() returns a Boolean value indicating whether the user is logged in or not

- get_full_name() returns the first name and the last name of the user, with a space in between

- `email_user(subject, message, from_email=None)` sends an email to the user
- `set_password(raw_password)` sets the user password to the passed value
- `check_password(raw_password)` returns a Boolean value indicating whether the passed password matches the user password

The names of these methods are self-explanatory. But one may wonder "Why is there a `set_password` method when one can just as easily set the password attribute of the user object?" To answer this question we need to examine the contents of the password field. Open the interactive console by running `python manage.py shell` and type the following statements:

```
>>> from django.contrib.auth.models import User
>>> user = User.objects.get(id=1)
>>> user.password
```

                    `'sha1$e1f02$bc3c0ef7d3e5e405cbaac0a44cb007c3d34c372c'`

You will receive a different string depending on your password, but it will be a long series of random-looking characters that is totally different from your actual password. What happened here? For security reasons, Django does not store your password in plain text in the database. Instead, it stores a hash value of your password. This hash is very difficult to reverse, but can still be used to verify the password when processing a login request. Remember when I said that implementing a session management system carries many caveats? Password storage is one of them, and Django handles it out of the box. You only need to remember to call the `set_password` method instead of directly accessing the password attribute, and the method will hash the password for you.

Enabling logout functionality

Now that we have a login page, the next step is providing a way for the user to log out. When the user hits the URL `logout/`, we will log the user out and redirect him or her back to the main page.

To do this, create a new view in the `bookmarks/views.py` file.

```
from django.http import HttpResponseRedirect
from django.contrib.auth import logout
def logout_page(request):
  logout(request)
  return HttpResponseRedirect('/')
```

The method almost reads as plain English. We use the `logout` method provided by `django.contrib.auth` to invalidate the user's session. Next, we redirect the user to the main page by returning an `HttpResponseRedirect` object. The constructor of this object takes the destination URL as a parameter.

Now we need to add a URL entry for this view. Open `urls.py` and create an entry as follows:

```
urlpatterns = patterns('',
    (r'^$', main_page),
    (r'^user/(\w+)/$', user_page),
    (r'^login/$', 'django.contrib.auth.views.login'),
    (r'^logout/$', logout_page),
)
```

That's it. To test the new view, make sure that you are logged in, and then hit `http://127.0.0.1:8000/logout/`. You will be redirected to the main page as an anonymous user.

To make the logout link accessible to the user, we need to edit all the templates that we have created so far and add a link to them. Even for a few templates, this is impractical for many reasons. To overcome this difficulty, we will restructure our templates by utilizing a feature called **template inheritance**.

Improving template structure

We have created three templates so far. They all share the same general structure, and only differ in the title and main content. Wouldn't it be great if we could factor out the shared sections into a single file so that if we want to modify all the pages in future, we will need to edit only one file?

Fortunately, the Django template system already provides such a feature-template inheritance. The idea is simple. We create a **base** template that contains the structure shared by all templates in the system. We also declare certain **blocks** of the base template so that they can be modified by **child** templates. Next, we create a template that **extends** the base template and modifies its blocks. The idea is very similar to class inheritance in object-oriented programming.

Let's apply this feature to our project. Create a file called `base.html` in the `templates` directory with the following content:

```
<!DOCTYPE html PUBLIC "-//W3C//DTD XHTML 1.0 Transitional//EN"
    "http://www.w3.org/TR/xhtml1/DTD/xhtml1-transitional.dtd">
<html>
<head>
```

```
    <title>
        Django Bookmarks | {% block title %}{% endblock %}
    </title>
</head>
<body>
    <h1>{% block head %}{% endblock %}</h1>
    {% block content %}{% endblock %}
</body>
</html>
```

The template utilizes a new template tag called `block`. This tag is used to define sections that are modifiable by child templates. Our base template contains three blocks, one for the title, one for the page heading, and one for the body.

To modify these blocks using a child template, edit the `templates/main_page.html` file and replace its content with the following:

```
{% extends "base.html" %}
{% block title %}Welcome to Django Bookmarks{% endblock %}
{% block head %}Welcome to Django Bookmarks{% endblock %}
{% block content %}
  {% if user.username %}
    <p>Welcome {{ user.username }}!
      Here you can store and share bookmarks!</p>
  {% else %}
    <p>Welcome anonymous user!
      You need to <a href="/login/">login</a>
      before you can store and share bookmarks.</p>
  {% endif %}
{% endblock %}
```

The new template of the main page starts by declaring that it extends the `base.html` file. This means that the `main_page.html` file is a child of the `base.html` file. It inherits its code and only changes blocks as required. Redefining a block in a child template isn't different from declaring it for the first time. The `main_page.html` file doesn't contain the general HTML structure any longer; it only redefines what it wants to redefine from the base template.

Next, let's restructure the `templates/user_page.html` file to make use of the new base template:

```
{% extends "base.html" %}
{% block title %}{{ username }}{% endblock %}
{% block head %}Bookmarks for {{ username }}{% endblock %}
{% block content %}
  {% if bookmarks %}
```

```
      <ul>
        {% for bookmark in bookmarks %}
          <li><a href="{{ bookmark.link.url }}">
            {{ bookmark.title }}</a></li>
        {% endfor %}
      </ul>
    {% else %}
      <p>No bookmarks found.</p>
    {% endif %}
{% endblock %}
```

Again, we simply redefine dynamic sections of the base template. The code that generates the bookmark listings is still exactly the same.

Finally, let's see how to convert the `templates/registration/login.html` file:

```
{% extends "base.html" %}
{% block title %}User Login{% endblock %}
{% block head %}User Login{% endblock %}
{% block content %}
  {% if form.has_errors %}
    <p>Your username and password didn't match.
      Please try again.</p>
  {% endif %}

  <form method="post" action=".">
    <p><label for="id_username">Username:</label>
      {{ form.username }}</p>
    <p><label for="id_password">Password:</label>
      {{ form.password }}</p>
    <input type="submit" value="login" />
    <input type="hidden" name="next" value="/" />
  </form>
{% endblock %}
```

Now that our templates have a common base, we can start improving our site's usability and appearance. Let's begin by adding a CSS stylesheet to the project. Stylesheets and images are static files and Django does not serve them. In a production environment, this task is left to the web server. But because we are currently using Django's development server, we will use a workaround to make it serve static content.

Open `urls.py`, and update it so that it looks as follows (the new code is highlighted):

```
import os
from django.conf.urls.defaults import *
from bookmarks.views import *
site_media = os.path.join(
```

```
    os.path.dirname(__file__), 'site_media'
)
urlpatterns = patterns('',
  (r'^$', main_page),
  (r'^user/(\w+)/$', user_page),
  (r'^login/$', 'django.contrib.auth.views.login'),
  (r'^logout/$', logout_page),
  (r'^site_media/(?P<path>.*)$', 'django.views.static.serve',
    {'document_root': site_media}),
)
```

The new entry binds all URLs under the site_media directory to Django's static file serving view. Unlike the previous URL entries, this one contains a third element. Some views have additional options that can be controlled by providing a dictionary as the third element in the view's URL entry. Here we are using this technique to tell the view where our static files are located.

Next, create a directory called site_media in your project directory. Inside it, create a blank file called style.css. Now, we will edit the templates/base.html file to link the stylesheet to the template and add a navigation menu:

```
<!DOCTYPE html PUBLIC "-//W3C//DTD XHTML 1.0 Transitional//EN"
    "http://www.w3.org/TR/xhtml1/DTD/xhtml1-transitional.dtd">
<html>
<head>
  <title>Django Bookmarks |
    {% block title %}{% endblock %}</title>
  <link rel="stylesheet" href="/site_media/style.css"
    type="text/css" />
</head>

<body>
  <div id="nav">
    <a href="/">home</a> |
    {% if user.is_authenticated %}
      welcome {{ user.username }}
      (<a href="/logout">logout</a>)
    {% else %}
      <a href="/login/">login</a>
    {% endif %}
  </div>
  <h1>{% block head %}{% endblock %}</h1>
  {% block content %}{% endblock %}
</body>
</html>
```

To correctly position the navigation menu on the page, edit the newly created stylesheet to add the following code:

```
#nav {
   float: right;
}
```

We are almost done. The navigation menu works well on the main page, but if you try the user_page view now, you will notice that the menu displays a login link whether you are logged in or not. This happens because the if condition in the navigation menu uses the user object to check the current user status. But this object isn't passed to the user_page.html template via the Context object. To overcome this problem, we have two options:

- Edit our user_page view and pass the user object to the template in it.
- Use a RequestContext object. This object is slightly different from normal Context objects. It automatically passes the user object to the template (along with several other variables). In order to do this, the RequestContext constructor takes the request object as its first parameter and a dictionary of template variables as the second parameter.

We will use the second approach because it is cleaner, as we will need to pass the user object to every template that we write in the future. Also, it is always better to factor out common code and reduce the amount of written code.

We will modify both main_page and user_page to use the RequestContext objects. Edit bookmarks/views.py, locate the main_page view, and modify it as in the following snippet:

```
from django.template import RequestContext

def main_page(request):
    return render_to_response(
        'main_page.html', RequestContext(request)
    )
```

As you can see, we do not need to pass request.user through the Context object any more. RequestContext handles this for us. Now rewrite the user_page view to use render_to_response and RequestContext:

```
def user_page(request, username):
    try:
        user = User.objects.get(username=username)
    except User.DoesNotExist:
        raise Http404('Requested user not found.')
    bookmarks = user.bookmark_set.all()
```

```
variables = RequestContext(request, {
  'username': username,
  'bookmarks': bookmarks
})
return render_to_response('user_page.html', variables)
```

The code for the views looks much more compact now. Although the restructuring of the templates took some time, the new structure will serve us better in the long term.

Our application now supports logging in and out. In the next section we are going to add user registration functionality.

User registration

The first user account was added to the database during the creation of our Django project. However, site visitors also need a method to create accounts on the site. User registration is a basic feature found in all social networking sites these days. We will create a user registration form in this section and, in the process, will also learn about the Django library that handles form generation and processing.

Django forms

Creating, validating, and processing forms is a very common task. Web applications receive input and collect data from users by means of web forms. So, naturally, Django comes with its own library to handle these forms. The Django form's library handles three common tasks:

- HTML form generation
- Server-side validation of user input
- HTML form redisplay in case of input errors

This library works in a way which is similar to the working of Django's data models. You start by defining a class that represents your form. This class must be derived from the `forms.Form` base class. Attributes in this class represent form fields. The `forms` package provides many field types, which is similar to how the `models` package provides many database types.

When you create an object from a class that is derived from the `forms.Form` base class, you can interact with it using a variety of methods. There are methods for HTML code generation, methods to access the input data, and methods to validate the form.

We will learn about the form's library by creating a user registration form in the next section.

Designing the user registration form

Let's start by creating our first Django form. Create a new file in the bookmarks application folder and call it forms.py. Then open the file in your code editor and enter the following code:

```
from django import forms
class RegistrationForm(forms.Form):
    username = forms.CharField(label=u'Username', max_length=30)
    email = forms.EmailField(label=u'Email')
    password1 = forms.CharField(
        label=u'Password',
        widget=forms.PasswordInput()
    )
    password2 = forms.CharField(
        label=u'Password (Again)',
        widget=forms.PasswordInput()
    )
```

After examining the code, you will notice that we defined this class in a way similar to how we defined the model classes. We derived the RegistrationForm class from forms.Form. All form classes need to inherit from this class. Next, we defined the fields that this form contains. There are many field types in the forms package. Several parameters are listed below, which can be passed to the constructor of any field type. Some specialized field types can take other parameters in addition to these:

- label: This parameter creates the label of the field when HTML code is generated.
- required: This parameter is set to true by default whether the user enters a value or not. To change it, pass required=False to the constructor.
- widget: This parameter lets you control how the field is rendered in HTML. We used it earlier to make the CharField of the password a password input field.
- help_text: This parameter displays description of the field when the form is rendered.

The following is a table of commonly used field types:

Field type	Description
CharField	Returns a string
IntegerField	Returns an integer
DateField	Returns a Python `datetime.date` object
DateTimeField	Returns a Python `datetime.datetime` object
EmailField	Returns a valid email address as a string
URLField	Returns a valid URL as a string

This is a partial list of available form widgets:

Widget type	Description
PasswordInput	A password text field
HiddenInput	A hidden input field
Textarea	A text area that enables text entry on multiple lines
FileInput	A file upload field

We can learn more about the form's API by experimenting in the interactive console. Run the console and issue the following commands:

```
$ python manage.py shell
>>> from bookmarks.forms import *
>>> form = RegistrationForm()
```

Now we have an instance of the `RegistrationForm` class. Let's see how it is rendered in HTML:

```
>>> print form.as_table()
```

This command will give you a long output in which you will see the HTML rendering of the form using table tags. You can also render the form using `ul` and `p` tags by calling `form.as_ul()` and `form.as_p()` respectively.

In addition, you can render individual form fields with the following code:

```
>>> print form['username']
  <input id="id_username" type="text" name="username" maxlength="30" />
```

Now that we know how to render the form, let's move to input validation. We can pass input to a form using its constructor:

```
>>> form = RegistrationForm({
...     'username': 'test',
...     'email': 'test@example.com',
...     'password1': 'test',
...     'password2': 'test'
... })
>>> form.is_valid()
        True
```

form.is_valid() returned True because all the fields were provided and the email address is valid. Now try to pass an invalid form field:

```
>>> form = RegistrationForm({
...     'username': 'test',
...     'email': 'invalid email',
...     'password1': 'test',
...     'password2': 'test'
... })
>>> form.is_valid()
        False
>>> form.errors
        {'email': [u'Enter a valid e-mail address.']}
```

Django did the form validation for us! You will get similar results if you do not pass a value for a field, because fields are required by default.

You can check whether a form has data or not using the form.is_bound attribute. If you try to validate an unbound form, you will get an exception. User input can be accessed through a dictionary at form.data, and if the form is valid, validated user input can be accessed at form.cleaned_data.

Now that you are comfortable with the forms.Form instances, we need to improve data validation for our form. The form in its current state detects missing fields and invalid email addresses, but we still need to do the following:

- Prevent the user from entering an invalid username or a username that's already in use
- Make sure that the two password fields match

Let's start with password validation because it's simpler. Open `bookmarks/forms.py` and append the following method to the `RegistrationForm` class:

```
def clean_password2(self):
  if 'password1' in self.cleaned_data:
    password1 = self.cleaned_data['password1']
    password2 = self.cleaned_data['password2']
    if password1 == password2:
      return password2
  raise forms.ValidationError('Passwords do not match.')
```

We will go through this code line by line:

- The method name is `clean_password2`. Custom validation methods always follow the format `clean_fieldname`.

- The method first checks whether `password1` passed validation. If the user enters a valid value for it, it will become accessible through the `self.cleaned_data` dictionary.

- Next, the method checks `password1` and `password2` for equality. If they are equal, it returns the clean value for `password2`. Here, we don't modify `password2` before returning it. But in other situations we may want to clean the value before returning it by stripping or escaping certain characters, for example.

- If validation fails, we raise an exception of the type `forms.ValidationError`. The constructor for this exception takes the error message as a parameter.

With password validation done, we will move to username validation. Add the following `import` statements at the beginning of `bookmarks/forms.py`:

```
import re
from django.contrib.auth.models import User
```

`re` is the regular expressions library. We will need it to make sure that the username doesn't contain invalid characters. We also import the `User` data model to check whether the entered username already exists or not.

Next, append the following method to `RegistrationForm`:

```
def clean_username(self):
  username = self.cleaned_data['username']
  if not re.search(r'^\w+$', username):
    raise forms.ValidationError('Username can only contain '
      'alphanumeric characters and the underscore.')
  try:
```

```
    User.objects.get(username=username)
except User.DoesNotExist:
  return username
raise forms.ValidationError('Username is already taken.')
```

Again, let's go through the method line by line:

- We first check the entered username against the regular expression ^\w+$. As you recall from Chapter 3, this is the same regular expression we used to capture the username from the user bookmarks URL. If the regular expression does not match the string, re.search returns None. In this case, we raise a ValidationError exception.
- If the username passes the first check, we search the User data model for a user with the same username. User.objects.get raises a DoesNotExist exception if it doesn't find a match. In this case, the username is new and we return it. Otherwise we raise an exception saying that the username is already taken.

You can experiment with these validation methods using the interactive console. Try to pass invalid data to the RegistrationForm constructor, and then check the errors dictionary for validation error messages. If you like, you can also implement a clean_ method for the email field to prevent a visitor from registering the same email address more than once.

We now have the registration form ready, but we still need a view and a template. Let's start with the view. Open bookmarks/views.py and insert the following code:

```
from bookmarks.forms import *
def register_page(request):
  if request.method == 'POST':
    form = RegistrationForm(request.POST)
    if form.is_valid():
      user = User.objects.create_user(
        username=form.cleaned_data['username'],
        password=form.cleaned_data['password1'],
        email=form.cleaned_data['email']
      )
      return HttpResponseRedirect('/')
  else:
    form = RegistrationForm()
  variables = RequestContext(request, {
      'form': form
  })
  return render_to_response(
    'registration/register.html',
    variables
  )
```

This view does one of the two things:

- If it's requested via the POST method, the user has submitted registration information. In this case, the view processes user input and redirects to the main page if everything goes well.

- Otherwise, the page generates HTML code for the registration form and renders a template called registration/register.html.

We retrieved user input from request.POST. This is a dictionary that contains POST input values. We pass this dictionary to the constructor of RegistrationForm using the call RegistrationForm(request.POST). This binds a form instance to the user input contained in the request.POST dictionary. Then, we can validate the input and redirect to the main page if everything is fine.

You may have noticed that a new user is created via User.objects.create_user instead of instantiating the User class. We used this approach because create_user takes care of password hashing for us (among several other things), so it's better to use it when creating new users.

If input validation fails, the form object will still be passed to the template. However, this form object will display helpful error messages to the user indicating what's wrong with the input.

Now we will move to the registration page template. Create a new file called templates/registration/register.html and add the following code to it:

```
{% extends "base.html" %}
{% block title %}User Registration{% endblock %}
{% block head %}User Registration{% endblock %}
{% block content %}
<form method="post" action=".">
  {{ form.as_p }}
  <input type="submit" value="register" />
</form>
{% endblock %}
```

Did you notice how compact and straightforward the view and template are? It's all because of the powerful and elegant Django forms library. The template simply renders the form using form.as_p, and adds a submit button below it.

Before we can test the registration view, we need to add a URL entry for it. Open urls.py and add the following line to the URL table:

```
(r'^register/$', register_page),
```

And we're done! Make sure that the development server is running, and navigate to `http://127.0.0.1:8000/register/`. The form should render and function correctly, but may look a bit messed up. To correct this, edit the stylesheet at `site_media` to add the following:

```
input {
   display: block;
}
```

It's much better now. Here is an image of the registration form:

Play with it. Try to enter invalid data and see how Django automatically generates error messages out of validation exceptions.

Now that we have a registration page, you may want to add a link to it in the site's navigation menu. Open `templates/base.html` and modify the navigation menu so that it looks like this:

```
<div id="nav">
  <a href="/">home</a> |
  {% if user.is_authenticated %}
    welcome {{ user.username }}
```

```
        (<a href="/logout">logout</a>)
    {% else %}
      <a href="/login/">login</a> |
      <a href="/register/">register</a>
    {% endif %}
</div>
```

One last thing: Wouldn't it be better if we displayed a success message after the user completes the registration process? Implementing this would be very simple. A view for such a page only loads and displays a template. It does not need to generate dynamic content or process input. Django already provides a view named `direct_to_template` in the `django.views.generic.simple` package for such a task, so let's use it.

Create a template, `register_success.html`, for the successful registration page at `templates/registration` with the following content:

```
{% extends "base.html" %}

{% block title %}Registration Successful{% endblock %}
{% block head %}
  Registration Completed Successfully
{% endblock %}

{% block content %}
  Thank you for registering. Your information has been
  saved in the database. Now you can either
  <a href="/login/">login</a> or go back to the
  <a href="/">main page</a>.
{% endblock %}
```

To directly link this template to a URL, first add this `import` statement at the beginning of `urls.py`:

```
from django.views.generic.simple import direct_to_template
```

Next, add the following entry to the URL table:

```
(r'^register/success/$', direct_to_template,
  {'template': 'registration/register_success.html'}),
```

Here the template name is passed to the view using a dictionary as a third item in the URL entry.

Finally, modify the `register_page` view in `bookmarks/views.py` so that it redirects to the new template upon successful registration. Search for the following statement:

```
return HttpResponseRedirect('/')
```

And replace it with this statement:

```
return HttpResponseRedirect('/register/success/')
```

That's it! To test the new template, you can either register a new username, or directly open this URL: `http://127.0.0.1:8000/register/success/`.

Account management

So far we have implemented session management and registration facilities. We now need to let the user update account information, such as the password or email address. To implement such features, we can do one of the two things:

- We can use the views that Django provides for common account management tasks as we did while creating the login form
- We can design our own form and process its input data as we did with the registration form

We've seen how to use both approaches. Each approach has its advantages and disadvantages. Obviously, designing your own form gives you greater control, but it requires more code. On the other hand, using a Django view is faster, but in this case you are limited to the form offered by Django. In the end, it's up to you to decide which approach to use.

I will summarize the views provided by the `django.contrib.auth` application. Each view expects a certain template name to be available and passes some variables to this template. Input handling is done inside the view, so you don't need to worry about it. All of the following views are available in the `django.contrib.auth. views` package:

- `logout`: Logs a user out and displays a template when done
- `logout_then_login`: Logs a user out and redirects to the login page
- `password_change`: Enables the user to change the password
- `password_change_done`: Is shown after the password is changed
- `password_reset`: Enables the user to reset the password and receive a new password via email
- `password_reset_done`: Is shown after the password is reset
- `redirect_to_login`: Redirects to the login page

These views are similar to the login view that we used at the beginning of the chapter. You can refer back to the online documentation of the `auth` application for usage details at `http://docs.djangoproject.com/en/dev/topics/auth/`.

With this information, we conclude this chapter. You now have a good understanding of the Django authentication system, and you should be able to implement session management and registration features in your own projects in the future.

Summary

In this chapter, you learned a lot about the user authentication and management system that comes with Django. This system provides features ranging from session handling to account maintenance. You used this system to allow the users of our social bookmarking application to register on the site and authenticate themselves by logging in. In the process, you learned about the Django form library and utilized it to build a registration form with input validation. You also learned how to derive templates from a base template, which is very important in organizing the site's structure and reusing the template code.

Here is a summary of the Django features covered in this chapter:

- The `User` object of the current user is accessible from the `request.user` attribute of the `HttpRequest` object passed to the view.

- As loading a template, rendering it, and wrapping it in an `HttpResponse` object is such a common task, Django provides a shortcut for it called `render_to_response`. This function is available from the `django.shortcuts` package.

- To set a user's password, don't access the `user.password` attribute directly. Instead, use the `user.set_password` method because it takes care of the password hashing for you.

- To render a form object, call the `as_table`, `as_p`, or `as_ul`. method on it.

- To bind a form to user input, pass user input as a dictionary to the form's constructor. To validate this input, check the `is_valid()` method and the `errors` attribute of the form object. Input data and clean data are accessible through `form.data` and `form.cleaned_data` attributes respectively.

- Custom field validation is done by adding a clean method to the form class. This method should be called `clean_fieldname`, and should return the cleaned value or raise a `forms.ValidationError` exception if input is invalid.

- To redirect the user from one view to another, return an `HttpResponseRedirect` object from the first view. This object's constructor takes the path of the second view as a parameter.

The next chapter brings many exciting features to our bookmarking application. We will build a form to enable users to post bookmarks to the site. The form will allow users to organize their bookmarks by using tags. Furthermore, we will let users browse popular tags in the database by using tag clouds. The next chapter contains a lot of interesting information, so keep reading!

5
Introducing Tags

Tags are one of the most prominent features in Web 2.0 applications. A tag is a keyword associated with a piece of information such as an article, an image, or a link. Tagging is a process of assigning tags to the content. It is usually done by the author or users, which allows for user-defined categorization of content. Tags have become very popular in web applications because they enable users to classify, view, and share content easily. If you are not familiar with tags, you can see some examples by visiting the social bookmarking service del.icio.us (at `http://del.icio.us/`) where tags are listed below bookmarks, or have a look at Wikipedia (at `http://en.wikipedia.org/`) where tags appear at the bottom of articles.

Since we are building a social bookmarking application, tags are vital for browsing and sharing bookmarks. To introduce tags into our system, we need a mechanism that enables users to submit bookmarks to the database along with tags. We also need a method for browsing bookmarks classified under a certain tag.

In this chapter, you will learn how to:

- Design a tag data model
- Build a bookmark submission form
- Create pages for listing bookmarks under a certain tag
- Build a tag cloud
- Restrict access to some pages
- Protect against malicious data input by users

The tag data model

Tags need to be stored in the database and must be associated with bookmarks. So, the first step in introducing tags to our project is creating a data model for tags. A tag object will only hold one piece of data—a string that represents the tag. In addition, we need to maintain a list of tags associated with a particular bookmark. You may recall from Chapter 3 that we used foreign keys to associate bookmarks with users, and called this a one-to-many relationship. However, the relationship between tags and bookmarks is not one-to-many because one tag can be associated with many bookmarks, and one bookmark can also have many tags associated with it. This is called a many-to-many relationship, and is represented in Django models using `models.ManyToManyField`.

You should be well aware by now that data models go into the `bookmarks/models.py` file, so open the file and add the following `Tag` class to it:

```
class Tag(models.Model):
    name = models.CharField(max_length=64, unique=True)
    bookmarks = models.ManyToManyField(Bookmark)
```

It's pretty straightforward, isn't it? We simply defined a data model for tags. This model holds the tag name and its bookmarks. When you finish entering the code, don't forget to run the following command in order to create a table for the model in the database:

```
$ python manage.py syncdb
```

Those who are already familiar with SQL know that many-to-many relationships are usually implemented in SQL by creating a third table that connects the two related tables. Let's see how Django implements this type of relationship. In the terminal, issue the following command:

```
$ python manage.py sql bookmarks
```

Here is the output, in which the new statements are highlighted:

```
BEGIN;
CREATE TABLE "bookmarks_link" (
  "id" integer NOT NULL PRIMARY KEY,
  "url" varchar(200) NOT NULL UNIQUE
);
CREATE TABLE "bookmarks_bookmark" (
  "id" integer NOT NULL PRIMARY KEY,
  "title" varchar(200) NOT NULL,
  "user_id" integer NOT NULL REFERENCES
    "auth_user" ("id"),
  "link_id" integer NOT NULL REFERENCES
```

```
        "bookmarks_link" ("id"),
    );
    CREATE TABLE "bookmarks_tag" (
        "id" integer NOT NULL PRIMARY KEY,
        "name" varchar(64) NOT NULL UNIQUE
    );
    CREATE TABLE "bookmarks_tag_bookmarks" (
        "id" integer NOT NULL PRIMARY KEY,
        "tag_id" integer NOT NULL
            REFERENCES "bookmarks_tag" ("id"),
        "bookmark_id" integer NOT NULL
            REFERENCES "bookmarks_bookmark" ("id"),
        UNIQUE ("tag_id", "bookmark_id")
    );
    COMMIT;
```

The output may slightly differ depending on your database engine.

Indeed, Django automatically creates an extra table called bookmarks_tag_bookmarks to maintain the many-to-many relationship.

It is worth noting that when we define a many-to-many relationship in Django model's API, the models.ManyToManyField can be placed in either of the two related models. We could have put this field in the Bookmark model instead of Tag, but since we created the Tag model later, we put the models.ManyToManyField in it.

Let's launch the interactive console and see the facilities offered by Django to work with many-to-many relationships:

```
$ python manage.py shell
>>> from bookmarks.models import *
>>> bookmark = Bookmark.objects.get(id=1)
>>> bookmark.link.url
        'http://www.packtpub.com/'
>>> tag1 = Tag(name='book')
>>> tag1.save()
>>> bookmark.tag_set.add(tag1)
>>> tag2 = Tag(name='publisher')
>>> tag2.save()
>>> bookmark.tag_set.add(tag2)
>>> bookmark.tag_set.all()
        [<Tag: Tag object>, <Tag: Tag object>]
```

So far we have created two tags and assigned them to a bookmark in our system. Though we didn't change the `Bookmark` data model, Django automatically added a new attribute to it called `tag_set` after creating the `Tag` model. This happened because of the many-to-many relationship we defined between `Bookmark` and `Tag`. Through this attribute we can access and manipulate tags assigned to a particular bookmark.

What about the list of bookmarks associated with a tag? It can be accessed through the `bookmarks` attribute in the `Tag` object. This attribute is named after the `models.ManyToManyField` that we defined in the `Tag` class:

```
>>> tag1.bookmarks.all()
        [<Bookmark: Bookmark object>]
```

Now we are able to assign tags to bookmarks and access the tags of a bookmark (and vice-versa). One little detail remains before we finish this section. When we print a data model object in the interactive console, such as a tag or bookmark, we get a generic string that doesn't help with identifying the object. It would be very helpful if we could override this output and replace it with a descriptive representation. Django provides a straightforward way to do this using a Python feature. If we simply define a method that takes no parameters called __unicode__ in our model, Django will use its output as the representation of the object. Let's add such a method to the `Tag` class. Open `bookmarks/models.py` and edit the class so that it looks as follows:

```
class Tag(models.Model):
    name = models.CharField(max_length=64, unique=True)
    bookmarks = models.ManyToManyField(Bookmark)
    def __unicode__(self):
      return self.name
```

To test this, open the interactive console and type the following:

```
>>> from bookmarks.models import *

>>> Tag.objects.all()
        [<Tag: book>, <Tag: publisher>]
```

It is much better now! These descriptive representations will greatly help us with developing and debugging our project, so let's do the same for the `Link` and `Bookmark` objects:

```
class Link(models.Model):
    url = models.URLField(unique=True)
    def __unicode__(self):
      return self.url
```

```
class Bookmark(models.Model):
    title = models.CharField(max_length=200)
    user = models.ForeignKey(User)
    link = models.ForeignKey(Link)
    def __unicode__(self):
        return u'%s, %s' % (self.user.username, self.link.url)
```

That's all there is to it. `User` objects already have custom `__unicode__` methods because the `User` data model is provided by Django.

Now that the data models are ready to store tagging information, we will move to the next step—designing a form that our users will use to submit bookmarks to the database.

How to use from X import *

Python style guidelines discourage the usage of this statement to import everything from a module. The reason behind this is to avoid cluttering the current namespace with unwanted classes and methods. In this book, I will use this statement for importing items from the modules that we will write on our own, since our modules are short and straightforward. But in larger projects, you may want to import specific items from modules to keep the namespace clean.

Creating the bookmark submission form

Now that we can store the tag data along with other bookmark information, we are ready to create a form for submitting bookmarks to the database. This form will let users specify the bookmark's URL, title, and tags. The process of creating this form is very similar to that of the registration form we created in Chapter 4. In fact, the method explained here can be used to create any HTML form that saves information into the database.

The first step in building our form is defining a class for it. So open the `bookmarks/forms.py` file and add the following class to it:

```
class BookmarkSaveForm(forms.Form):
    url = forms.URLField(
        label=u'URL',
        widget=forms.TextInput(attrs={'size': 64})
    )
    title = forms.CharField(
        label=u'Title',
        widget=forms.TextInput(attrs={'size': 64})
    )
```

```
tags = forms.CharField(
  label=u'Tags',
  required=False,
  widget=forms.TextInput(attrs={'size': 64})
)
```

This code should look familiar to you. For each field, we specified a label and a widget. We changed the default widget of `models.CharField` in order to control the size of the text field. (Remember that widgets are used to control how a field is rendered.) The HTML attributes of a field can be changed by passing a dictionary of attribute names and values to the widget constructor. Here we specified a size of 64 for text fields.

By specifying correct field types in our form, we don't have to implement any additional input validation. For example, Django will automatically make sure that the user enters a valid URL because the corresponding field is defined as `models.URLField`.

It's worth noting that we used a simple text field for tags. Users can enter the bookmark's tags by typing them into this field and separating them with spaces. This method is used by many Web 2.0 applications and can be improved with AJAX, as we will see in the next chapter.

Next, we will create a view for our form. Again, the view will be very similar to the registration view we wrote earlier. Create a new view called `bookmark_save_page` in the `bookmarks/views.py` file with the following code:

```
from bookmarks.models import *

def bookmark_save_page(request):
  if request.method == 'POST':
    form = BookmarkSaveForm(request.POST)
    if form.is_valid():
      # Create or get link.
      link, dummy = Link.objects.get_or_create(
        url=form.cleaned_data['url']
      )
      # Create or get bookmark.
      bookmark, created = Bookmark.objects.get_or_create(
        user=request.user,
        link=link
      )
      # Update bookmark title.
      bookmark.title = form.cleaned_data['title']
      # If the bookmark is being updated, clear old tag list.
      if not created:
        bookmark.tag_set.clear()
```

```
        # Create new tag list.
        tag_names = form.cleaned_data['tags'].split()
        for tag_name in tag_names:
          tag, dummy = Tag.objects.get_or_create(name=tag_name)
          bookmark.tag_set.add(tag)
        # Save bookmark to database.
        bookmark.save()
        return HttpResponseRedirect(
          '/user/%s/' % request.user.username
        )
    else:
      form = BookmarkSaveForm()
    variables = RequestContext(request, {
      'form': form
    })
    return render_to_response('bookmark_save.html', variables)
```

This view has the same structure as the registration view. However, it uses a different form and template, and contains a different method for storing information into the database. Let's go through the code line by line:

- This view may be requested using GET or POST. If it's a GET request, a BookmarkSaveForm is created and passed to the template.

- If the request method is POST, input data is passed to a BookmarkSaveForm object for validation and processing.

- If the input is valid, we build a corresponding Bookmark object and save it in the database. Each bookmark consists of a user, a link, a title, and some tags. Let's see how we get each one of these:

  ○ The User object is already available at request.user.

  ○ To get the Link object, we use a method called Link.objects.get_or_create. This is the first time we have used this method, but it will prove to be very useful while working with Django forms. This method works as its name suggests. It tries to get an object from the database according to the parameters it receives. If it cannot find such an object, it creates a new one and saves it to the database. It returns the retrieved or created object and a Boolean flag indicating whether the object was created or not. Because we don't care whether the Link object was created or was already available, we store this flag in a dummy variable that we will not use later.

  ○ Title and tags are provided by the user and are accessible through form.cleaned_data.

- Now that we have all the required elements, we proceed to build the `Bookmark` object. This is also done using `get_or_create`. The reason is that the user may submit the same URL more than once. Since we don't want to store the same bookmark twice in the database, we use `get_or_create`. If it's a new bookmark, a new object is created and saved. Otherwise, the already existing bookmark is retrieved and updated.

- A title is given to the bookmark by assigning the title string to the `bookmark.title` attribute.

- If the bookmark was not created, it means that it already has a list of tags associated with it. So we have to clear it before assigning a new tag list to the bookmark.

- Finally, we split the tags string and iterate through it adding each tag to the bookmark's tag set. `Tag` objects are also retrieved or created using `get_or_create`.

- The view terminates either by rendering the form through a template called `bookmark_save.html` or it terminates after saving a submitted bookmark, in which case the user is redirected to his or her page.

As you can see, the view is a bit long. But it is easy to understand if you break it up into sections.

Before we see the view in action, we need to write a template and add a new URL entry for it. The template will be almost identical to the registration template, as all that it does is to display the form that it receives from the view. Create a file called `bookmark_save.html` in the `templates` folder and insert the following code into it:

```
{% extends "base.html" %}
{% block title %}Save Bookmark{% endblock %}
{% block head %}Save Bookmark{% endblock %}
{% block content %}
<form method="post" action=".">
  {{ form.as_p }}
  <input type="submit" value="save" />
</form>
{% endblock %}
```

We are almost there. Open the `urls.py` file and insert the following entry in it:

```
(r'^save/$', bookmark_save_page),
```

You may have noticed that our URL table is growing fast. It is a good idea to reorganize it a bit with comments and whitespaces. Here is one suggested method in which we could do this:

```
urlpatterns = patterns('',
    # Browsing
    (r'^$', main_page),
    (r'^user/(\w+)/$', user_page),

    # Session management
    (r'^login/$', 'django.contrib.auth.views.login'),
    (r'^logout/$', logout_page),
    (r'^register/$', register_page),
    (r'^register/success/$', direct_to_template,
        {'template': 'registration/register_success.html'}),

    # Account management
    (r'^save/$', bookmark_save_page),

    # Site media
    (r'^site_media/(?P<path>.*)$', 'django.views.static.serve',
        {'document_root': site_media}),
)
```

And we have finished. Launch the development server, make sure that you are logged in, and navigate to http://127.0.0.1:8000/save/. You will see the bookmark submission form:

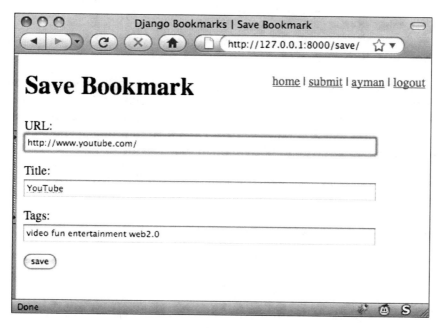

Try to submit links and notice how they are added to your user page. You can also try submitting an invalid URL and see how Django requests a valid one before proceeding. .

Because we programmed the user page in Chapter 4, tags will not be visible on the user page, even though they are stored in the database. We will correct this in the next section when we add a page for browsing all bookmarks under a certain tag. But before we continue, there are two issues that need addressing—creating a link to the bookmark submission form in the navigation menu, and restricting it to logged-in users.

Restricting access to logged-in users

Let's add a link to the bookmark submission form in the navigation menu and restructure the menu a little. Open the `templates/base.html` file and update it so that it looks as follows (changes are highlighted):

```
<div id="nav">
    <a href="/">home</a> |
    {% if user.is_authenticated %}
      <a href="/save/">submit</a> |
      <a href="/user/{{ user.username }}/">
        {{ user.username }}</a> |
      <a href="/logout/">logout</a>
    {% else %}
      <a href="/login/">login</a> |
      <a href="/register/">register</a>
    {% endif %}
</div>
```

Did you notice that we made sure we are logged in before submitting a bookmark? This is because bookmarks are associated with `User` objects, and we don't want anonymous users to save bookmarks without identifying themselves first. But how do we make sure that anonymous users cannot submit links? There are many methods, two of which will be explained here.

As we have seen in the previous chapter, you can see if the current user is logged in by using `request.user.is_authenticated()`. So, if we wrap the `bookmark_save_page` view with an `if` condition such as the following, we can see whether the user is logged in or not:

```
if request.user.is_authenticated():
  # Process form.
else:
  # Redirect to log-in page.
```

However, the task of limiting certain pages to logged-in users is so common that Django provides a shortcut for it, and it turns out that this shortcut is even easier to use. Therefore, it is recommended that you use this shortcut rather than the one above. Add it to the `bookmark_save_page` section of the `views.py` file:

```
from django.contrib.auth.decorators import login_required
@login_required
def bookmark_save_page(request):
```

This is all that we need to do in order to limit a view to logged-in users. We first import a method called `login_required` from `django.contrib.auth.decorators` and then apply it to our view. The syntax that we used to do this may look new to you. It is called **decorator** syntax. A Python decorator is a function that modifies another function. Here we modify the `bookmark_save_page` using the `login_required` decorator. The decorator checks whether the user is logged in before passing control to the view.

One little detail remains. How will `login_required` know our login URL? By default, it assumes that the page is located at `/accounts/login/`. If we want to change this, we can store the login URL in a variable called `LOGIN_URL`. This variable resides in the `settings.py` file. Add the following code at the end of the `settings.py` file:

```
LOGIN_URL = '/login/'
```

Now, log out and try to navigate directly to `http://127.0.0.1:8000/save/`. You will be automatically redirected to the login form.

The natural step after letting users submit bookmarks is providing methods for browsing these bookmarks. In a previous chapter, we built a simple user page that lists all of the user's bookmarks. In the next section we will improve this page and add another page for browsing the bookmarks under a certain tag.

Methods for browsing bookmarks

Browsing bookmarks lies at the heart of our application. Therefore, it is vital to provide a variety of ways for the user to explore available bookmarks and share them with others.

Although we intend to provide several ways to browse bookmarks, the technique used to generate bookmark listings will remain the same.

1. First, we build a list of bookmarks using the Django model API.

2. Next, we present the list of bookmarks using a template.

Although the details of how to build the bookmark list differ from one page to another, bookmark listing pages will often look similar. We can present each bookmark as a link, with a tag and user information below it. It would be a good idea if we could write one template and reuse it across all the pages. Template inheritance, which we learned about in the previous chapter, is one method that can be used to achieve this. However, the Django template system provides another powerful mechanism that we will learn about in this section. It is called the `include` template tag.

The concept of the `include` tag is simple. It lets you include the contents of one template file in another. It's similar to copying the contents of one template and pasting it into another. Let's see the tag in action by writing a generic template for a bookmark list. Create a new file called `bookmark_list.html` in the `templates` directory and enter the following code into it:

```
{% if bookmarks %}
  <ul class="bookmarks">
    {% for bookmark in bookmarks %}
      <li>
        <a href="{{ bookmark.link.url }}" class="title">
          {{ bookmark.title }}</a>
        <br />
        {% if show_tags %}
          Tags:
          {% if bookmark.tag_set.all %}
            <ul class="tags">
              {% for tag in bookmark.tag_set.all %}
                <li>{{ tag.name }}</li>
              {% endfor %}
            </ul>
          {% else %}
            None.
          {% endif %}
          <br />
        {% endif %}
        {% if show_user %}
          Posted by:
          <a href="/user/{{ bookmark.user.username }}/"
            class="username">
            {{ bookmark.user.username }}</a>
        {% endif %}
      </li>
    {% endfor %}
```

```
  </ul>
{% else %}
  <p>No bookmarks found.</p>
{% endif %}
```

If you recall how we created bookmark listings on user pages, you will notice that this piece of code does something very similar. Let's see how it works:

- The code first checks whether `bookmarks` is empty or not. If it contains items, the code enters a loop and iterates through all the bookmarks. Otherwise, it prints a message saying that no bookmarks were found and exits.

- In the body of the main `for` loop, the code prints a link to the bookmark and then enters another loop to print the bookmark's tags. To give us greater control over list rendering, we check whether a variable named `show_tags` is true before printing tags.

- Finally, we check whether a variable named `show_user` is true. If it is, we print a link to the user's page.

The Boolean variable `show_*` will prove to be very useful later on, because it enables us to control how the list looks from within the view by passing flags to the list template. For example, when displaying a user's bookmarks, there is no point in displaying a link to the user page, because we are already viewing it. Furthermore, we added CSS classes to the list elements which simplify styling the list later on.

Improving the user page

Now to make use of this template snippet on the user page, we need to include it from within the `user_page.html` template. So open the `templates/user_page.html` file and modify it to look like the following (the modified section is highlighted):

```
{% extends "base.html" %}
{% block title %}{{ username }}{% endblock %}
{% block head %}Bookmarks for {{ username }}{% endblock %}
{% block content %}
  {% include "bookmark_list.html" %}
{% endblock %}
```

It is clear how simple the template has become! We had to modify the content block and include the `bookmark_list.html` template in it. This would work as we had copied and pasted the code of `bookmark_list.html` into the block. The main benefit of this feature is that we can reuse `bookmark_list.html` somewhere else in the project by including it in another template (for example, when generating a tag page).

Before we can see the new template in action, we need to modify the user view and our stylesheet a little. On the user page, we want to display a tag list but not the username. The current user_page view does not pass any show_* flags to the template. Since an undeclared Boolean variable is considered False by Django templates, we need to set show_tags to True in the user_page view. Open bookmarks/views.py and change the view as follows:

```
from django.shortcuts import get_object_or_404
def user_page(request, username):
    user = get_object_or_404(User, username=username)
    bookmarks = user.bookmark_set.order_by('-id')
    variables = RequestContext(request, {
        'bookmarks': bookmarks,
        'username': username,
        'show_tags': True
    })
    return render_to_response('user_page.html', variables)
```

The highlighted lines here indicate the new additions to this section of code. We have added show_tags to the template variable list and changed the logic that retrieves the user object. Here we used another Django shortcut called get_object_or_404. This function does exactly what the old code did; it tries to get an object from the provided model according to the passed arguments. If it succeeds, it returns the corresponding object; otherwise, it raises a **Page not found (404)** error. The task of rendering a page that represents an object in the database or returning a 404 error is very common, so this was the best time to learn about a shortcut for it.

We have also changed how the bookmark list is retrieved. Instead of calling the all method, we used the order_by method which orders the entries according to the column name provided as an argument to the method. If the column name is preceded by a - sign, the sorting order becomes descending instead of ascending. We do this because we want the more recent links to appear at the top of the page.

To improve the look of the tag list and avoid nested lists, open the site_media/style.css file and insert the following:

```
ul.tags, ul.tags li {
    display: inline;
    margin: 0;
    padding: 0;
}
```

This CSS snippet declares tag lists and their items to be inline, which looks much better and saves space on the page.

Try out the improved user page at `http://127.0.0.1:8000/user/` `your_username/`. You will see bookmark tags below the links.

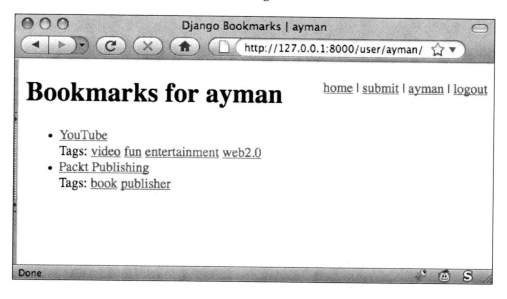

Creating a tag page

Next, we will create a similar bookmark listing for tags. For this task, we won't write any new code. We will basically sew together the components that we wrote when we created the user page.

Let's start by adding a URL entry for the tag page. Open the `urls.py` file and insert the following entry (preferably below the user page entry so as to keep the table organized):

```
(r'^tag/([^\s]+)/$', tag_page),
```

The captured part of this regular expression differs from that of the user page. We only allow alphanumeric characters in usernames. But for tags, any non-whitespace character is allowed because users may want to use characters such as + and & in their tags. In regular expressions, `\s` matches any whitespace character by putting it in a character class (a set of characters between brackets) and preceding it with ^. By doing this, we negate what the character class matches. In other words, `[abc]` matches either a, b, or c, whereas `[^abc]` matches any character except a, b, and c. Therefore, `[^\s]` matches any character except for whitespaces, which is exactly what we want.

Next, we will create the `tag_page` view. Open `bookmarks/views.py` and insert the following code:

```
def tag_page(request, tag_name):
  tag = get_object_or_404(Tag, name=tag_name)
  bookmarks = tag.bookmarks.order_by('-id')
  variables = RequestContext(request, {
    'bookmarks': bookmarks,
    'tag_name': tag_name,
    'show_tags': True,
    'show_user': True
  })
  return render_to_response('tag_page.html', variables)
```

This time, the code is almost identical in structure to that of the `user_page` view. We are dealing with tags instead of users, but otherwise the code is essentially the same.

Lastly, we need to create a template for the tag page. Create a file called `templates/tag_page.html` with the following contents:

```
{% extends "base.html" %}
{% block title %}Tag: {{ tag_name }}{% endblock %}
{% block head %}Bookmarks for tag: {{ tag_name }}{% endblock%}
{% block content %}
  {% include "bookmark_list.html" %}
{% endblock %}
```

Again, the template is essentially the same as `user_page.html`. Here we include `bookmark_list.html` to generate the actual list. See how we managed to add a new feature to our application in a few minutes and with only a few lines of code? This was possible because we took advantage of Django's features to modularize and reuse our code.

Before we try out the new tag page, we will link tag names to their respective tag pages. To do this, open `bookmark_list.html` and modify the section that generates tag lists as follows:

```
<ul class="tags">
  {% for tag in bookmark.tag_set.all %}
    <li>
      <a href="/tag/{{ tag.name }}/">{{ tag.name }}</a>
    </li>
  {% endfor %}
</ul>
```

Changes will be automatically applied to user and tag pages. This is another benefit of the `include` tag. We didn't have to modify each template separately.

Now, navigate to your user page and click one of the tags to see the tag page in action:

Nice, isn't it? With this, we have finished creating tag pages. The users of our application now have many more, and better, ways to browse available bookmarks.

Building a tag cloud

The last feature that we are going to implement in this chapter is tag clouds. A tag cloud is a visual representation of the tags available in a system and of how often they are used. The size of a tag name in the cloud corresponds to the number of items under this tag. The more the items under a certain tag, the larger the font size used to represent the tag. The tag cloud is a quick and convenient way to form an idea of what content is available on the site and browse it.

The key to implementing a tag cloud is building a list of tags along with the number of items associated with each tag. We will call this number the count of the tag. Next, we find the minimum and maximum counts among all tags. After that, we assign a weight to every tag based on where the count is located between the minimum and maximum. The closer to the maximum, the larger the weight.

Let's code this. Open the `bookmarks/views.py` file and create a new view for the tag cloud page:

```python
def tag_cloud_page(request):
    MAX_WEIGHT = 5
    tags = Tag.objects.order_by('name')
    # Calculate tag, min and max counts.
    min_count = max_count = tags[0].bookmarks.count()
    for tag in tags:
        tag.count = tag.bookmarks.count()
        if tag.count < min_count:
            min_count = tag.count
        if max_count < tag.count:
            max_count = tag.count
    # Calculate count range. Avoid dividing by zero.
    range = float(max_count - min_count)
    if range == 0.0:
        range = 1.0
    # Calculate tag weights.
    for tag in tags:
        tag.weight = int(
            MAX_WEIGHT * (tag.count - min_count) / range
        )
    variables = RequestContext(request, {
        'tags': tags
    })
    return render_to_response('tag_cloud_page.html', variables)
```

Let's go through each section of this code:

- We retrieve a list of all tags sorted by name. `MAX_WEIGHT` holds the maximum weight that can be generated. If it's set to 5, we will get weights between 0 and 5.

- We iterate through the list, find the number of bookmarks associated with each tag, and cache this number in a temporary attribute called `count`. We also calculate the minimum and maximum counts, and maintain them in `min_count` and `max_count` respectively.

- We calculate the difference between `max_count` and `min_count`. If it's zero, we set it to 1.0 to avoid dividing by zero.

- We iterate through tags once again and assign a weight to each tag. Weight is calculated by finding how far the current tag's count is from the minimum count and dividing this value by range. To get an integer, we multiply the result (which will be between 0.0 and 1.0) by the number of weights, and convert to an integer.

- Finally, we pass the resulting tag list to a template called
  tag_cloud_page.html.

Let's move to writing the template. Create a file called tag_cloud_page.html in the
templates directory with the following content:

```
{% extends "base.html" %}
{% block title %}Tag Cloud{% endblock %}
{% block head %}Tag Cloud{% endblock %}
{% block content %}
  <div id="tag-cloud">
    {% for tag in tags %}
      <a href="/tag/{{ tag.name }}/"
        class="tag-cloud-{{ tag.weight }}">
          {{ tag.name }}</a>
    {% endfor %}
  </div>
{% endblock %}
```

As you can see, the template simply loops through the tags, creates links out of them, and assigns a CSS class to each tag based on its weight.

Next, we will write CSS code to style the tag cloud. Open the site_media/style.css file and insert the following code:

```
#tag-cloud {
   text-align: center;
}
#tag-cloud a {
   margin: 0 0.2em;
}
.tag-cloud-0 { font-size: 100%; }
.tag-cloud-1 { font-size: 120%; }
.tag-cloud-2 { font-size: 140%; }
.tag-cloud-3 { font-size: 160%; }
.tag-cloud-4 { font-size: 180%; }
.tag-cloud-5 { font-size: 200%; }
```

Finally, add an entry to the `urls.py` file. We will map `tag_cloud_page` to the URL `/tag/` (without a tag name after it):

```
(r'^tag/$', tag_cloud_page),
```

We are done! Navigate to `http://127.0.0.1:8000/tag/` to see the results. The page depends on how many bookmarks you have in the database. Here is a screenshot of the page after entering a lot of bookmarks:

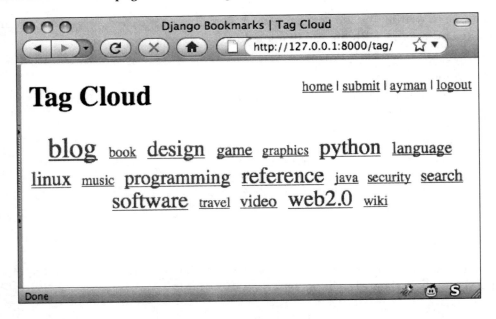

A word on security

At the beginning of this chapter, we designed a web form that accepts user input, stores it in the database, and presents it to the visitors of the site. Since our application will be open to the public, anyone can register and submit whatever data they want. Therefore, we need to take certain precautions to handle the situation in which malicious data is supplied.

The golden rule in web development is "Do not trust user input, ever." You must always validate and sanitize user input before saving it to the database and presenting it in HTML pages. In this section, we will discuss how to achieve this and how to avoid two common vulnerabilities in web applications.

SQL injection

One of the most common attacks on web applications is SQL injection, in which the attacker uses certain techniques to manipulate SQL queries and obtain data or store malicious data into the database. SQL injection vulnerabilities happen when the developer uses input to construct SQL queries without escaping special characters in it. As we are using the Django model API to store and retrieve data, we are safe from these types of attacks. The model API automatically escapes input before using it to build queries. So we do not need to do anything special to protect our application from SQL injections.

Cross-Site Scripting (XSS)

Another common web attack is Cross-Site Scripting, in which a malicious user supplies JavaScript code within input. When this input is rendered into an HTML page, the JavaScript code is executed to take control of the page and steal information such as cookies. To protect against such attacks, user input must always be escaped or sanitized before being presented in a page. Again, Django automatically does this for us by escaping template variables before printing them to a page.

Let's verify that this feature actually works in our project. The bookmark submission form allows any string to be entered and stored in the database as the title of a bookmark. For example, a user may submit the following string as a bookmark title:

```
<script>alert("Test.");</script>
```

This string is a JavaScript code that displays a message box with the text Test. Our application will accept it as a bookmark title and store it in the database. The model API will automatically escape special characters before saving it to the database, and everything will run as expected. Furthermore, when a user opens a page that contains this bookmark, the title will be escaped and printed to the page. This prevents the JavaScript code from being executed. Try it so that you can see for yourself how Django protects our application from two most common attacks.

There are times, however, when you want to disable auto-escaping. Let's say you have a piece of HTML-formatted text that has already been sanitized and you don't want Django to escape it. Fortunately, Django provides a feature called **template filters** to process variables before printing them in a template. One of these filters is the safe filter which disables auto-escaping and prints the template variable as is. Another useful filter is urlencode which escapes a string for use in a URL. This is different from the default method of escaping.

Let's use the `urlencode` filter in the `templates/bookmark_list.html` file. Open the file and modify it as follows:

```
[...]
{% if show_tags %}
  Tags:
  {% if bookmark.tag_set.all %}
    <ul class="tags">
    {% for tag in bookmark.tag_set.all %}
      <li><a href="/tag/{{ tag.name|urlencode }}/">
        {{ tag.name }}</a></li>
    {% endfor %}
    </ul>
  {% else %}
    None.
  {% endif %}
  <br />
{% endif %}
[...]
```

The syntax for applying a filter is similar to the one for shell pipes in UNIX or Linux. A template filter is a Python function. When a filter is applied to a variable, the variable is passed to the filter as an argument and the return value of the filter is used in the output of the template. Here, `tag.name` is passed to the `urlencode` filter before printing, which properly encodes the tag name as part of a URL.

Auto-escaping works by replacing special characters, such as < and > with their HTML entities `&lt;` and `&gt;` respectively. The entity `&lt` tells the browser to display a < instead of interpreting it as a tag opening. On the other hand, the `urlencode` filter replaces < with `%3C`, which is the proper way of embedding this character in a URL.

You will need to do a similar change to `templates/tag_cloud_page.html` file:

```
{% extends "base.html" %}
{% block title %}Tag Cloud{% endblock %}
{% block head %}Tag Cloud{% endblock %}
{% block content %}
  <div id="tag-cloud">
    {% for tag in tags %}
      <a href="/tag/{{ tag.name|urlencode }}/"
        class="tag-cloud-{{ tag.weight }}">
        {{ tag.name }}</a>
    {% endfor %}
  </div>
{% endblock %}
```

To sum up, always keep in mind that Django auto-escapes template variables. To disable this for a particular variable, use the `safe` template filter. To encode a variable that is part of a URL, use the `urlencode` filter.

Summary

With this, we conclude the chapter. We implemented many important features for our application and learned several new Django features. We started by creating a data model for storing tags, and then created a form for bookmark submission. After that, we built pages that allow users to browse and discover new bookmarks.

Here is a quick summary of the Django features mentioned in this chapter:

- In the data model API, many-to-many relationships are represented with `models.ManyToManyField`. Django automatically generates attributes to access the items associated with a particular object through this relationship.

- To customize the string representation of a data model, provide a method called `__unicode__` in the model's class. This method takes no parameters and should return your preferred representation.

- To customize a form field, supply a custom widget. The widget constructor takes a dictionary of HTML attributes and their values as its parameters.

- The `objects` attribute of a data model provides a very useful method called `get_or_create`. This method retrieves an object from the database according to the passed arguments or creates one if it doesn't exist.

- To restrict a view to logged-in users, use the `login_required` decorator. You may also need to override the default login path, which is stored in the `LOGIN_URL` variable.

- The `include` template tag is a valuable feature for reusing template snippets on multiple pages.

- To protect your application against XSS attacks, use the `escape` and `urlencode` template filters. The `escape` filter escapes HTML characters in input and uses it when building HTML output; whereas the `urlencode` filter escapes input for use in a URL.

In the next chapter, we will improve the bookmark submission form and other parts of the application with JavaScript and AJAX. It is going to be a fun chapter with lots of new information and technologies to learn, so keep reading!

6
Enhancing the User Interface with AJAX

The coming of AJAX was an important landmark in the history of Web 2.0. AJAX is a group of technologies that enables developers to build interactive, feature-rich web applications. Most of these technologies were available many years before AJAX too. However, the advent of AJAX represents the transition of the web from static pages that need to be refreshed whenever data was exchanged to dynamic, responsive, and interactive user interfaces.

Since our project is a Web 2.0 application, it should be heavily focused on the user's experience. The success of our application depends on getting users to post and share content on it. Therefore, the user interface of our application is one of our major concerns. This chapter will improve the interface of our application by introducing AJAX features, making it more user-friendly and interactive.

In this chapter, you will learn about the following:

- AJAX and the benefits of using it in web applications
- How to install an AJAX framework in Django
- How to use the open source jQuery framework
- Live searching of bookmarks
- Editing a bookmark in place without loading a separate page
- Auto-completion of tags when submitting a bookmark

AJAX and its advantages

AJAX, which stands for **Asynchronous JavaScript** and **XML**, consists of the following technologies:

- HTML and CSS for structuring and styling information.
- JavaScript for accessing and manipulating information dynamically.
- `XMLHttpRequest` — an object provided by modern browsers for exchanging data with the server without reloading the current web page.
- A format for transferring data between the client and the server. XML is sometimes used, but it could be HTML, plain text, or a JavaScript-based format known as JSON.

AJAX technologies allow the code on the client-side to exchange data with the server behind the scenes, without having to reload the entire page each time the user makes a request. Using AJAX, web developers are able to increase the interactivity and usability of web pages.

AJAX offers the following advantages when implemented in the right places:

- **Better user experience**: With AJAX the user can do a lot without refreshing the page, which brings web applications closer to regular desktop applications.
- **Better performance**: By exchanging only the required data with the server, AJAX saves bandwidth and increases the application's speed.

There are numerous examples of web applications that use AJAX. Google Maps and Gmail are perhaps two of the most prominent examples. In fact, these two applications played an important role in spreading the adoption of AJAX because of the success they enjoyed. What sets Gmail apart from other web mail services is its user interface, which enables users to manage their emails interactively without waiting for a page reload after every action. This creates a better user experience and makes Gmail feel like a responsive and feature-rich application rather than a simple web site.

This chapter explains how to use AJAX with Django so as to make our application more responsive and user-friendly. We are going to implement three of the most common AJAX features found in web applications today. But before that we will learn about the benefits of using an AJAX framework as opposed to working with raw JavaScript functions.

Using an AJAX framework in Django

In this section we will choose and install an AJAX framework in our application. This step isn't entirely necessary when using AJAX in Django, but can greatly simplify working with AJAX. There are many advantages in using an AJAX framework:

- JavaScript implementations vary from browser to browser. Some browsers provide more complete and feature-rich implementations, whereas others contain implementations that are incomplete or don't adhere to standards. Without an AJAX framework, the developer must keep track of browser support for the JavaScript features that they are using and work around the limitations that are present in some browser implementations of JavaScript. On the other hand, when using an AJAX framework, the framework takes care of this for us. It abstracts access to the JavaScript implementation and deals with the differences and quirks of JavaScript across browsers. This way, we can concentrate on developing features instead of worrying about browser differences and limitations.

- The standard set of JavaScript functions and classes is a bit lacking for fully fledged web application development. Various common tasks require many lines of code even though they could have been wrapped in simple functions. Therefore, even if you decide not to use an AJAX framework, you will find yourself having to write a library of functions that encapsulates JavaScript facilities and makes them more usable. But why reinvent the wheel when there are many excellent open source libraries already available?

AJAX frameworks available in the market today range from comprehensive solutions that provide server-side and client-side components to lightweight client-side libraries that simplify working with JavaScript. Given that we are already using Django on the server-side, we only want a client-side framework. In addition, the framework should be easy to integrate with Django without requiring additional dependencies. And finally, it is preferable to pick a light and fast framework. There are many excellent frameworks that fulfill our requirements. For our application, I'm going to pick jQuery because it's the lightest. It also enjoys a very active development community and a wide range of plug-ins. If you already have experience with another framework, you can continue using it during this chapter. It is true that you will have to adapt the JavaScript code in this chapter to your framework, but Django code on the server-side will remain the same no matter which framework you choose.

Now that you know the benefits of using an AJAX framework, we will move to installing jQuery into our project.

Downloading and installing jQuery

One of the advantages of jQuery is that it consists of a single lightweight file. To download it, head to http://jquery.com/ and choose the latest version (1.2.6 at the time of writing). You will find two choices:

- **Uncompressed version**: This is the standard version that I recommend you to use during development. You will get a .js file with the library's code in it.

- **Compressed version**: You will also get a .js file if you download this version. However, the code will look obfuscated. jQuery developers produce this version by applying many operations on the uncompressed .js file to reduce its size, such as removing whitespaces and renaming variables, as well as many other techniques. This version is useful when you deploy your application because it offers exactly the same features as the uncompressed one, but with a smaller file size.

I recommend the uncompressed version during development because you may want to look into jQuery's code and see how a particular method works. However, the two versions offer exactly the same set of features, and switching from one to another is just a matter of replacing one file.

Once you have the jquery-xyz.js file (where xyz is the version number), rename it to jquery.js, and copy it to the site_media directory of our project. (Remember that this directory holds static files which are not Python code.) Next, you will have to include this file in the base template of our site. This will make jQuery available to all of our project pages. To do so, open the templates/base.html file and add the highlighted code to its head section:

```
<head>
  <title>Django Bookmarks |
    {% block title %}{% endblock %}</title>
  <link rel="stylesheet" href="/site_media/style.css"
    type="text/css" />
  <script type="text/javascript"
  src="/site_media/jquery.js"></script>
</head>
```

To add your own JavaScript code to an HTML page, you can either put the code in a separate .js file and link it to the HTML page using the script tag just shown, or write the code directly in the body of a script tag:

```
<script type="text/javascript">
  // JavaScript code goes here.
</script>
```

However, the first method is recommended over the second one, because it helps keep the source tree organized by putting HTML and JavaScript code in different files. Since we are going to write our own .js files during this chapter, we need a way to link the .js files to the templates without having to edit the base.html template every time. We will do this by creating a template block in the head section of the base.html template. When a particular page wants to include its own JavaScript code, this block may be overridden to add the relevant script tag to the page. We will call this block external because it is used to link external files to pages. Open the templates/base.html file and modify its head section as follows:

```html
<head>
  <title>Django Bookmarks |
    {% block title %}{% endblock %}</title>
  <link rel="stylesheet" href="/site_media/style.css"
    type="text/css"/>
  <script type="text/javascript" src="/site_media/jquery.js">
  </script>
    {% block external %}{% endblock %}
</head>
```

It's done. From now on, when a view wants to use some JavaScript code, it can link a JavaScript file to its template by overriding the external template block.

Before we start to implement AJAX enhancements in our project, let's go through a quick introduction to the jQuery framework.

The jQuery JavaScript framework

jQuery is a library of JavaScript functions that facilitates interacting with HTML documents and manipulating them. The library is designed to reduce the time and effort spent on writing code and achieving cross-browser compatibility. At the same time, it takes full advantage of what JavaScript offers to build interactive and responsive web applications.

The general workflow of using jQuery consists of two steps:

1. Select an HTML element or a group of elements to work on.
2. Apply a jQuery method to the selected group.

Element selectors

jQuery provides a simple approach to select elements. It works by passing a CSS selector string to a function called $. Here are some examples to illustrate the usage of this function:

- If you want to select all anchor (`<a>`) elements on a page, you can use the function call $(`"a"`)
- If you want to select anchor elements which have the `.title` CSS class, use $(`"a.title"`)
- To select an element whose ID is `#nav`, you can use $(`"#nav"`)
- To select all list item (`<li>`) elements inside `#nav`, use $(`"#nav li"`)

And so on. The $() function constructs and returns a jQuery object. After that, you can call methods on this object to interact with the selected HTML elements.

jQuery methods

jQuery offers a variety of methods to manipulate HTML documents. You can hide or show elements, attach event handlers to events, modify CSS properties, manipulate the page structure and, most importantly, perform AJAX requests.

Before we go through some of the most important methods, I highly recommend using the Firefox web browser and an extension called Firebug to experiment with jQuery. This extension provides a JavaScript console that is very similar to the interactive Python console. With it, you can enter JavaScript statements and see their output directly without creating and editing the files. To obtain Firebug, go to `http://www.getfirebug.com/`, and click on the **INSTALL FIREBUG** link. Depending on the security settings of Firefox, you may need to approve the web site as a safe source of extensions.

If you don't want to use Firefox or Firebug, Firebug's web site offers a "lite" version of the extension for other browsers in the form of a JavaScript file. Download the file to the `site_media` directory, and then include it in the `templates/base.html` template as we did with `jquery.js`, which is shown as follows:

```
<head>
  <title>Django Bookmarks | {% block title %}{% endblock %}</title>
  <link rel="stylesheet" href="/site_media/style.css"
        type="text/css"/>
    <script type="text/javascript" src="/site_media/firebug.js">
    </script>
  <script type="text/javascript" src="/site_media/jquery.js">
  </script>
  {% block external %}{% endblock %}
</head>
```

To experiment with the methods outlined in this section, launch the development server and navigate to the application's main page. Open the Firebug console by pressing *F12*, and try selecting elements and manipulating them.

Hiding and showing elements

Let's start with something simple. To hide an element on the page, call the `hide()` method on it. To show it again, call the `show()` method. For example, try this on the navigation menu of your application:

```
>>> $("#nav").hide()
>>> $("#nav").show()
```

As you can see in the following figure, Firebug works just like the interactive Python console:

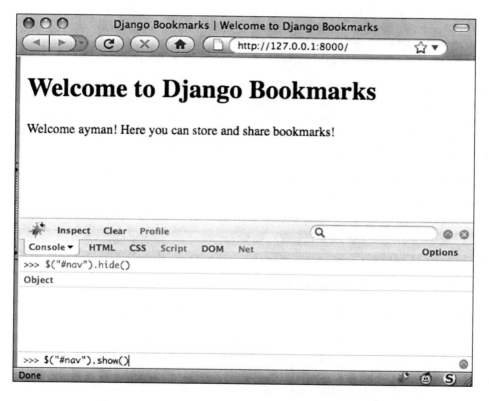

You can also animate the element while hiding and showing it. Try the `fadeOut()`, `fadeIn()`, `slideUp()`, or `slideDown()` method to see two of these animated effects.

These methods (like all other jQuery methods) also work if you select more than one element at once. For example, if you open your user page and enter the following method call into the Firebug console, all of the tags will disappear:

```
>>> $('.tags').slideUp()
```

Accessing CSS properties and HTML attributes

Next, we will learn how to change CSS properties of elements. jQuery offers a method called `css()` for performing CSS operations. If you call this method with a CSS property name passed as a string, it returns the value of this property:

```
>>> $("#nav").css("display")
        Result: "block"
```

If you pass a second argument to this method, it sets the specified CSS property of the selected element to the additional argument:

```
>>> $("#nav").css("font-size", "0.8em")
        Result: <div id="nav" style="font-size: 0.8em;">
```

In fact, you can manipulate any HTML attribute and not just CSS properties. To do so, use the `attr()` method which works in a way similar to `css()`. Calling it with an attribute name returns the attribute value, whereas calling it with an attribute name/ value pair sets the attribute to the passed value. To test this, go to the bookmark submission form and enter the following into the console:

```
>>> $("input").attr("size", "48")
        Results:
        <input id="id_url" type="text" size="48" name="url">
        <input id="id_title" type="text" size="48" name="title">
        <input id="id_tags" type="text" size="48" name="tags">
```

(The output may slightly differ depending on the Firebug version.)

This will at once change the sizes of all input elements on the page to 48.

In addition, there are shortcut methods to get and set commonly used attributes such as `val()`, which returns the value of an input field when called without arguments, and sets this value to an argument, if you pass one. There is also `html()` which controls the HTML code inside an element. Finally, there are two methods that can be used to attach or detach a CSS class to an element. They are called `addClass()` and `removeClass()`. A third method is provided to toggle a CSS class, which is called `toggleClass()`. All of these class methods take the name of the class to be changed as a parameter.

Manipulating HTML documents

Now that you are comfortable with manipulating HTML elements, let's see how to add new elements or remove existing elements. To insert HTML code before an element, use the `before()` method. To insert code after an element, use the `after()` method. Notice how jQuery methods are well-named and very easy to remember!

Let's test these methods by inserting parentheses around tag lists on the user page. Open your user page and enter the following in the Firebug console:

```
>>> $(".tags").before("<strong>(</strong>")
>>> $(".tags").after("<strong>)</strong>")
```

You can pass any string you want to—`before()` or `after()`. The string may contain plain text, one HTML element, or more. These methods offer a very flexible way to dynamically add HTML elements to an HTML document.

If you want to remove an element, use the `remove()` method. For example:

```
$("#nav").remove()
```

Not only does this method hide the element, it also removes it completely from the document tree. If you try to select the element again after using the `remove()` method, you will get an empty set:

```
>>> $("#nav")
     Result: []
```

Of course, this only removes the elements from the current instance of the page. If you reload the page, the elements will appear again.

Traversing the document tree

Although CSS selectors offer a very powerful way to select elements, there are times when you want to traverse the document tree starting from a particular element. For this, jQuery provides several methods. The `parent()` method returns the parent of the currently selected element. The `children()` method returns all the immediate children of the selected element. Finally, the `find()` method returns all the descendants of the currently selected element. All of these methods take an optional CSS selector string to limit the result to elements that match the selector. For example, `$("#nav").find("a")` returns all the `<a>` descendants of #nav.

If you want to access an individual element of a group, use the `get()` method which takes the index of the element as a parameter. For example, `$("li").get(0)` returns the first `<li>` element out of the selected group.

Handling events

Next, we will learn about handling events. An event handler is a JavaScript function that is invoked when a particular event happens, for example when a button is clicked or a form is submitted. jQuery provides a large set of methods to attach handlers to events — events of particular interest in our application are mouse clicks and form submissions. To handle the event of clicking on an element, we select this element and call the `click()` method on it. This method takes an event handler function as a parameter. Let's try this using the Firebug console. Open the main page of the application, and insert a button after the welcome message:

```
>>> $("p").after("<button id=\"test-button\">Click me!</button>")
```

(Notice that we had to escape the quotations in the strings passed to the `after()` method.)

If you try to click this button, nothing will happen. So let's attach an event handler to it:

```
>>> $("#test-button").click(function () { alert("You clicked me!"); })
```

Now, when you click the button, a message box will appear. How did this work? The argument that we passed to `click()` may look a bit complicated, so let's examine it again:

```
function () { alert("You clicked me!"); }
```

This appears to be a function declaration, but without a function name. Indeed, this construct creates what is called an anonymous function in JavaScript terminology. It is used when you need to create a function on the fly and pass it as an argument to another function. We could have avoided using anonymous functions and declared the event handler as a regular function:

```
>>> function click_handler() { alert("You clicked me!"); }
>>> $("#test-button").click(click_handler)
```

This code achieves the same effect, but the first one is more concise and compact. I highly recommend you to get used to anonymous functions in JavaScript (if you are not already), as I'm sure you will appreciate this construct and find it more readable after using it for a while.

Handling form submissions is very similar to handling mouse clicks. First, you select the form, and then you call the `submit()` method on it and pass the handler as an argument. We will use this method many times while adding AJAX features to our project in later sections.

Sending AJAX requests

Before we finish this section, let's talk about AJAX requests. jQuery provides many ways to send AJAX requests to the server. There is, for example, the `load()` method which takes a URL and loads the page at this URL into the selected element. There are also methods for sending `GET` or `POST` requests and receiving the results. We will examine these methods in more depth while implementing AJAX features in our project.

What next?

This wraps up our quick introduction to jQuery. The information provided in this section will be enough to continue with this chapter. Once you finish the chapter, you will be able to implement many interesting AJAX features on your own. But please keep in mind that this jQuery introduction is only the tip of the iceberg. If you want a comprehensive treatment of the jQuery framework, I highly recommend the book *Learning jQuery* from Packt Publishing, as it covers jQuery in much more detail. You can find out more about the book at:

```
http://www.packtpub.com/jQuery
```

Implementing live searching of bookmarks

We will start introducing AJAX into our application by implementing live searching. The idea behind this feature is simple: When the user types a few keywords into a text field and clicks **search**, JavaScript works behind the scenes to fetch search results and presents them on the same page. The search page does not reload, thus saving bandwidth and providing a better and more responsive user experience.

Before we start implementing this, we need to keep in mind an important rule while working with AJAX: Write your application so that it works without AJAX, and then introduce AJAX to it. If you do so, you ensure that everyone will be able to use your application, including users who don't have JavaScript enabled and those who use browsers without AJAX support.

Implementing basic searching

So before we work with AJAX, let's write a simple view that searches bookmarks by title. First of all, we need to create a search form. So, open `bookmarks/forms.py` and add the following class to it:

```
class SearchForm(forms.Form):
    query = forms.CharField(
        label=u'Enter a keyword to search for',
        widget=forms.TextInput(attrs={'size': 32})
    )
```

As you can see, it's a pretty straightforward `form` class with only one text field. This field will be used by the user to enter search keywords.

Next, let's create a view for searching. Open the `bookmarks/views.py` file and enter the following code into it:

```
def search_page(request):
    form = SearchForm()
    bookmarks = []
    show_results = False
    if 'query' in request.GET:
        show_results = True
        query = request.GET['query'].strip()
        if query:
            form = SearchForm({'query' : query})
            bookmarks = Bookmark.objects.filter(
                title__icontains=query
            )[:10]
    variables = RequestContext(request, {
        'form': form,
        'bookmarks': bookmarks,
        'show_results': show_results,
        'show_tags': True,
        'show_user': True,
    })
    return render_to_response('search.html', variables)
```

Apart from a couple of method calls, the view should be very easy to understand. We first initialize three variables: `form` which holds the search form, `bookmarks` which holds the bookmarks that we will display in the search results, and `show_results` which is a Boolean flag. We use this flag to distinguish between two cases:

- The search page was requested without a search query. In this case, we shouldn't display any search results, not even a **No bookmarks found** message.

- The search page was requested with a search query. In this case, we display the search results, or a **No bookmarks found** message if the query does not match any bookmarks.

We need the `show_results` flag because the `bookmarks` variable alone is not enough to distinguish between the above two cases. `bookmarks` will be empty when the search page is requested without a query, and it will also be empty when the query does not match any bookmarks.

Next, we check whether a query was sent by checking, if the `request.GET` dictionary has a key named `'query'`:

```
if 'query' in request.GET:
    show_results = True
    query = request.GET['query'].strip()
    if query:
        form = SearchForm({'query' : query})
        bookmarks = Bookmark.objects.filter(
            title__icontains=query
        )[:10]
```

We use GET instead of POST here because the search form does not create or change the data; it merely queries the database. The general rule is to use GET with forms that query the database, and POST with forms that create, change, or delete records from the database.

If a query is submitted by the user, we set `show_results` to `True` and call `strip()` on the query string to ensure that it contains non-whitespace characters before we proceed with searching. If this is indeed the case, we bind the form to the query and retrieve a list of bookmarks that contain the query in their title. Searching is done by using a method called `filter` in `Bookmark.objects`. This is the first time that we have used this method; you can think of it as the equivalent of a SELECT statement in Django models. It receives the search criteria in its arguments and returns search results. The name of each argument must adhere to the following naming convention:

`field__operator`

Note that `field` and `operator` are separated by two underscores: `field` is the name of the field that we want to search by, and `operator` is the lookup method that we want to use. Here is a list of the commonly-used operators:

- `exact`: The value of the argument is an exact match of the field
- `contains`: The field contains the value of the argument
- `startswith`: The field starts with the value of the argument

- lt: The field is less than the value of the argument
- gt: The field is greater than the value of the argument

Also, there are case-insensitive versions of the first three operators: iexact, icontains, and istartswith.

After this explanation of the filter method, let's get back to our search view. We use the icontains operator to get a list of bookmarks that match the query and retrieve the first 10 items using Python's list-slicing syntax. Finally, we pass all the variables to a template called search.html to render the search page.

Now create the search.html template in the templates directory with the following content:

```
{% extends "base.html" %}
{% block title %}Search Bookmarks{% endblock %}
{% block head %}Search Bookmarks{% endblock %}
{% block content %}
<form id="search-form" method="get" action=".">
  {{ form.as_p }}
  <input type="submit" value="search" />
</form>
<div id="search-results">
  {% if show_results %}
    {% include "bookmark_list.html" %}
  {% endif %}
</div>
{% endblock %}
```

The template consists of familiar aspects that we have used before. We build the results list by including bookmark_list.html, like we did when building the user and tag pages. We gave an ID to the search form and rendered the search results in a div identified by another ID so that we can interact with them using JavaScript later. Notice how many times the include template tag saved us from writing additional code? It also lets us modify the look of the bookmarks list by editing a single file. This Django template feature is indeed very helpful in organizing and managing templates.

Before you test the new view, add an entry for it in the urls.py file:

```
urlpatterns = patterns('',
    # Browsing
    (r'^$', main_page),
    (r'^user/(\w+)/$', user_page),
    (r'^tag/([^\s]+)/$', tag_page),
```

```
    (r'^tag/$', tag_cloud_page),
    (r'^search/$', search_page),
    [...]
)
```

Test the search view by navigating to `http://127.0.0.1:8000/search/` and experiment with it. You can also add a link to it in the navigation menu if you want. Just edit `templates/base.html` and add the highlighted code:

```
<div id="nav">
  <a href="/">home</a> |
  {% if user.is_authenticated %}
    <a href="/save/">submit</a> |
    <a href="/search/">search</a> |
    <a href="/user/{{ user.username }}/">
      {{ user.username }}</a> |
    <a href="/logout/">logout</a>
  {% else %}
    <a href="/login/">login</a> |
    <a href="/register/">register</a>
  {% endif %}
</div>
```

We now have a functional (albeit very basic) search page. The search functionality itself will be improved during later chapters, but what matters to us is introducing AJAX to the search form so that results are fetched behind the scenes and presented to the user without reloading the page. Thanks to our modular code, the task will turn out to be much simpler than it may seem.

Implementing live searching

To implement live searching, we need to do two things:

- Intercept and handle the event of submitting the search form. This can be done using the `submit()` method of jQuery.

- Use AJAX to load the search results in the back scenes, and insert them into the page. This can be done using the `load()` method of jQuery as we will see next.

Let's focus on the method called `load()`. jQuery offers this method that retrieves a page from the server and inserts its contents into the selected element. In its simplest form, the function takes the URL of the remote page to be loaded as a parameter.

First of all, let's modify our search view a little so that it only returns search results without the rest of the search page when it receives an additional GET variable called ajax. We do so to enable JavaScript code on the client-side to easily retrieve search results without the rest of the search page HTML. This can be done by simply using the bookmark_list.html template instead of the search.html template when request.GET contains the key ajax. Open the bookmarks/views.py file and modify search_page (towards the end) so that it becomes as follows:

```
def search_page(request):
  [...]
  variables = RequestContext(request, {
    'form': form,
    'bookmarks': bookmarks,
    'show_results': show_results,
    'show_tags': True,
    'show_user': True
  })
  if request.GET.has_key('ajax'):
    return render_to_response('bookmark_list.html', variables)
  else:
    return render_to_response('search.html', variables)
```

Next, create a file called search.js in the site_media directory and link it to the templates/search.html template like this:

```
{% extends "base.html" %}
{% block external %}
  <script type="text/javascript"
    src="/site_media/search.js"></script>
{% endblock %}
{% block title %}Search Bookmarks{% endblock %}
{% block head %}Search Bookmarks{% endblock %}
[...]
```

Now for the fun part! Let's create a function that loads search results and inserts them into the corresponding div. Write the following code into the site_media/search.js file:

```
function search_submit() {
  var query = $("#id_query").val();
  $("#search-results").load(
    "/search/?ajax&query=" + encodeURIComponent(query)
  );
  return false;
}
```

Let's go through this function line by line:

- The function first gets the query string from the text field using the `val()` method.

- We use the `load()` method to get search results from the `search_page` view, and insert the search results into the `#search-results` div. The request URL is constructed by first calling `encodeURIComponent` on `query`, which works exactly like the `urlencode` filter we used in Django templates. Calling this function is important to ensure that the constructed URL remains valid even if the user enters special characters into the text field such as `&`. After escaping `query`, we concatenate it with `/search/?ajax&query=`. This URL invokes the `search_page` view and passes the `GET` variables `ajax` and `query` to it. The view returns search results, and the `load()` method in turn loads the results into the `#search-results` div.

- We return `false` from the function to tell the browser not to submit the form after calling our handler. If we don't return `false` in the function, the browser will continue to submit the form as usual, and we don't want that.

One little detail remains: Where and when to attach `search_submit` to the submit event of the search form? A rule of a thumb when writing JavaScript is that we cannot manipulate elements in the document tree before the document finishes loading. Therefore, our function must be invoked as soon as the search page is loaded. Fortunately for us, jQuery provides a method to execute a function when the HTML document is loaded. Let's utilize it by appending the following code to the `site_media/search.js` file:

```
$(document).ready(function () {
  $("#search-form").submit(search_submit);
});
```

`$(document)` selects the document element of the current page. Notice that there are no quotations around `document`. It's a variable provided by the browser, not by a string. `ready()` is a method that takes a function and executes it as soon as the selected element finishes loading. So in effect, we are telling jQuery to execute the passed function as soon as the HTML document is loaded. We pass an anonymous function to the `ready()` method. This function simply binds `search_submit` to the submit event of the form `#search-form`.

That's it. We've implemented live searching with less than 15 lines of code. To test the new functionality, navigate to `http://127.0.0.1:8000/search/`, submit queries, and notice how the results are displayed without reloading the page.

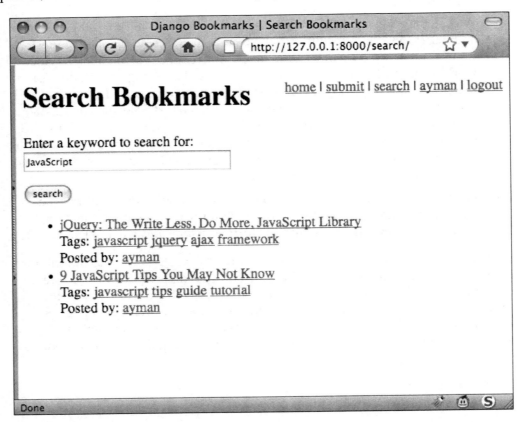

The information covered in this section can be applied to any form that needs to be processed in the back scenes without reloading the page. You can, for example, create a comment form with a preview button that loads the preview in the same page without reloading it. In the next section, we will enhance the user page to let users edit their bookmarks in place, without navigating away from the user page.

Editing bookmarks in place

Editing of posted content is a very common task in web sites. It's usually implemented by offering an edit link next to content. When clicked, this link takes the user to a form located on another page where content can be edited. When the user submits the form, he or she is redirected back to the content page.

Imagine, on the other hand, that you could edit content without navigating away from the content page. When you click on edit, the content is replaced with a form. When you submit the form, it disappears and the updated content appears in its place. Everything happens on the same page. Edit form rendering and submission are done using JavaScript and AJAX. Wouldn't such a workflow be more intuitive and responsive?

The technique described above is called **in-place editing**. It is now finding its way into web applications and becoming more common. We will implement this feature in our application by letting the user edit his or her bookmarks in place on the user page.

Since our application doesn't support the editing of bookmarks yet, we will implement this first and then modify the editing procedure to work in place.

Implementing basic bookmark editing

We already have most of the parts that are needed to implement bookmark editing. If you recall from the previous chapter, in the `bookmarks/views.py` file, we implemented the `bookmark_save_page` view in such a way that if the user tries to save the same URL more than once, the same bookmark is updated rather than duplicated. This was easy to do, thanks to the `get_or_create` method provided by data models. This little detail greatly simplifies the implementation of bookmark editing. Here is what we need to do:

1. We pass the URL of the bookmark that we want to edit as a GET variable named `url` to the `bookmark_save_page` view.

2. We modify `bookmark_save_page` so that it populates the fields of the bookmark form if it receives the GET variable. The form is populated with the data of the bookmark that corresponds to the passed URL.

When the populated form is submitted, the bookmark will be updated as explained earlier, because it will look as if the user submitted the same URL another time.

Before we implement the technique just described, let's reduce the size of `bookmark_save_page` by moving the part that saves a bookmark to a separate function. We will call this function `_bookmark_save`. The underscore at the beginning of the name tells Python not to import this function when the views module is imported. The function expects a request and a valid form object as parameters; it saves a bookmark out of the form data, and returns this bookmark.

Open the `bookmarks/views.py` file and create the following function. You can cut and paste the code from `bookmark_save_page` if you like, as we are not making any changes to it except for the return statement at the end.

```python
def _bookmark_save(request, form):
  # Create or get link.
  link, dummy = Link.objects.get_or_create(
    url=form.cleaned_data['url']
  )
  # Create or get bookmark.
  bookmark, created = Bookmark.objects.get_or_create(
    user=request.user,
    link=link
  )
  # Update bookmark title.
  bookmark.title = form.cleaned_data['title']
  # If the bookmark is being updated, clear old tag list.
  if not created:
    bookmark.tag_set.clear()
  # Create new tag list.
  tag_names = form.cleaned_data['tags'].split()
  for tag_name in tag_names:
    tag, dummy = Tag.objects.get_or_create(name=tag_name)
    bookmark.tag_set.add(tag)
  # Save boojkmark to database and return it.
  bookmark.save()
  return bookmark
```

Now in the same file replace the code that you removed from `bookmark_save_page` with a call to `_bookmark_save`:

```python
@login_required
def bookmark_save_page(request):
  if request.method == 'POST':
    form = BookmarkSaveForm(request.POST)
    if form.is_valid():
      bookmark = _bookmark_save(request, form)
      return HttpResponseRedirect(
        '/user/%s/' % request.user.username
      )
  else:
    form = BookmarkSaveForm()
  variables = RequestContext(request, {
    'form': form
  })
  return render_to_response('bookmark_save.html', variables)
```

The current logic in `bookmark_save_page` works like this:

```
if there is POST data:
  Validate and save bookmark.
  Redirect to user page.
else:
  Create an empty form.
Render page.
```

To implement bookmark editing, we need to slightly modify the logic as follows:

```
if there is POST data:
  Validate and save bookmark.
  Redirect to user page.
else if there is a URL in GET data:
  Create a form and populate it with the URL's bookmark.
else:
  Create an empty form.
Render page.
```

Let's translate the above pseudo code into Python. Modify `bookmark_save_page` in the `bookmarks/views.py` file so that it looks like the following (new code is highlighted):

```python
@login_required
def bookmark_save_page(request):
    if request.method == 'POST':
        form = BookmarkSaveForm(request.POST)
        if form.is_valid():
            bookmark = _bookmark_save(request, form)
            return HttpResponseRedirect(
                '/user/%s/' % request.user.username
            )
    elif 'url' in request.GET:
        url = request.GET['url']
        title = ''
        tags = ''
        try:
            link = Link.objects.get(url=url)
            bookmark = Bookmark.objects.get(
                link=link,
                user=request.user
            )
            title = bookmark.title
            tags = ' '.join(
                tag.name for tag in bookmark.tag_set.all()
```

```
        )
    except (Link.DoesNotExist, Bookmark.DoesNotExist):
        pass
    form = BookmarkSaveForm({
        'url': url,
        'title': title,
        'tags': tags
    })
else:
    form = BookmarkSaveForm()
variables = RequestContext(request, {
    'form': form
})
return render_to_response('bookmark_save.html', variables)
```

This new section of the code first checks whether a GET variable called url exists. If this is the case, it loads the corresponding Link and Bookmark objects of this URL, and binds all the data to a bookmark saving form. You may wonder why we load the Link and Bookmark objects in a try-except construct that silently ignores exceptions. Indeed, it's perfectly valid to raise an Http404 exception if no bookmark was found for the requested URL, but our code chooses to only populate the URL field in this situation, leaving the title and tags fields empty.

Now, let's add edit links next to each bookmark in the user page. Open the templates/bookmark_list.html template and insert the highlighted code:

```
{% if bookmarks %}
  <ul class="bookmarks">
    {% for bookmark in bookmarks %}
      <li>
        <a href="{{ bookmark.link.url }}" class="title">
          {{ bookmark.title }}</a>
        {% if show_edit %}
        <a href="/save/?url={{ bookmark.link.url|urlencode }}"
          class="edit">[edit]</a>
        {% endif %}
        <br />
        {% if show_tags %}
          Tags:
          {% if bookmark.tag_set.all %}
            <ul class="tags">
              {% for tag in bookmark.tag_set.all %}
                <li><a href="/tag/{{ tag.name|urlencode }}/">
                  {{ tag.name|escape }}</a></li>
              {% endfor %}
```

```
        </ul>
      {% else %}
         None.
      {% endif %}
      <br />
 [...]
```

Notice how we constructed the edit links by appending the bookmark's URL to /save/?url=. Also, since we only want to show edit links on the user's page, the template renders these links only when the show_edit flag is set to True. Otherwise, it wouldn't make sense to let the user edit other people's links. Now open the bookmarks/views.py file and add the show_edit flag to template variables in user_page:

```
def user_page(request, username):
  user = get_object_or_404(User, username=username)
  bookmarks = user.bookmark_set.order_by('-id')
  variables = RequestContext(request, {
    'bookmarks': bookmarks,
    'username': username,
    'show_tags': True,
    'show_edit': username == request.user.username,
  })
  return render_to_response('user_page.html', variables)
```

The expression username == request.user.username evaluates to True only when the user is viewing his or her own page, and this is precisely what we want.

Finally, I suggest reducing the font size of edit links a little. Open the site_media/style.css file and append the following to its end:

```
ul.bookmarks .edit {
  font-size: 70%;
}
```

And we are done! Feel free to navigate to your user page and experiment with editing your bookmarks before we continue.

Implementing in-place editing of bookmarks

Now that we have bookmark-editing implemented, let's move to the exciting part—adding in-place editing with AJAX!

Our approach to this task will be as follows:

- We intercept the event of clicking on an edit link and use AJAX to load a bookmark editing form from the server. Then we replace the bookmark on the page with the editing form.

- When the user submits the edit form, we intercept the submission event and use AJAX to send the updated bookmark to the server. The server saves the bookmark and returns the HTML representation of the new bookmark. We replace the edit form on the page with the markup returned by the server.

We will implement the above using an approach very similar to live searching. First we modify bookmark_save_page so that it responds to AJAX requests when a GET variable called ajax exists. Next, we write JavaScript code to retrieve an edit form from the view, which posts bookmark data back to the server when the user submits this form.

Since we want to return the markup of an edit form to the AJAX script from the bookmark_save_page view, let's restructure our templates a little. Create a file called bookmark_save_form.html in templates, and move the bookmark saving form from bookmark_save.html to this new file:

```html
<form id="save-form" method="post" action="/save/">
  {{ form.as_p }}
  <input type="submit" value="save" />
</form>
```

Notice that we also changed the action attribute of the form to /save/ and gave it an ID. This is necessary for the form to work on the user page as well as on the bookmark submission page.

Next, include this new template in the bookmark_save.html file:

```html
{% extends "base.html" %}
{% block title %}Save Bookmark{% endblock %}
{% block head %}Save Bookmark{% endblock %}
{% block content %}
{% include "bookmark_save_form.html" %}
{% endblock %}
```

OK, now we have the form in a separate template. Let's update the bookmark_save_page view to handle both normal and AJAX requests. Open the bookmarks/views.py file and update the view to look like the following (new lines are highlighted):

```python
@login_required
def bookmark_save_page(request):
    ajax = 'ajax' in request.GET
```

```
    if request.method == 'POST':
      form = BookmarkSaveForm(request.POST)
      if form.is_valid():
        bookmark = _bookmark_save(form)
        if ajax:
          variables = RequestContext(request, {
            'bookmarks': [bookmark],
            'show_edit': True,
            'show_tags': True
            })
          return render_to_response(
            'bookmark_list.html', variables
          )
        else:
          return HttpResponseRedirect(
            '/user/%s/' % request.user.username
          )
      else:
        if ajax:
          return HttpResponse(u'failure')
  elif 'url' in request.GET:
    url = request.GET['url']
    title = ''
    tags = ''
    try:
      link = Link.objects.get(url=url)
      bookmark = Bookmark.objects.get(
        link=link, user=request.user
      )
      title = bookmark.title
      tags = ' '.join(
        tag.name for tag in bookmark.tag_set.all()
      )
    except (Link.DoesNotExist, Bookmark.DoesNotExist):
      pass
    form = BookmarkSaveForm({
      'url': url,
      'title': title,
      'tags': tags
    })
  else:
    form = BookmarkSaveForm()
  variables = RequestContext(request, {
    'form': form
```

```
    })
  if ajax:
    return render_to_response(
      'bookmark_save_form.html',
      variables
    )
  else:
    return render_to_response(
      'bookmark_save.html',
      variables
    )
```

Let's examine each highlighted section separately:

```
ajax = request.GET.has_key('ajax')
```

At the beginning of the method, we check whether a GET variable named ajax exists. We store the result of the check in a variable called ajax. Later in the method, we can check whether we are handling an AJAX request or not by using this variable in an if condition:

```
if form.is_valid():
  bookmark = _bookmark_save(form)
  if ajax:
    variables = RequestContext(request, {
          'bookmarks': [bookmark],
          'show_edit': True,
          'show_tags': True
          })
    return render_to_response('bookmark_list.html', variables)
  else:
    return HttpResponseRedirect(
      '/user/%s/' % request.user.username
    )
else:
  if ajax:
    return HttpResponse('failure')
```

If we receive a POST request, we check whether the submitted form is valid or not. If it is valid, we save the bookmark. Next we check if this is an Ajax request. If it is, we render the saved bookmark using the bookmark_list.html template and return it to the requesting script. Otherwise, it is a normal form submission and so we redirect the user to their user page. On the other hand, if the form is not valid, we only act if it's an AJAX request by returning the string "failure", which we will respond to by displaying an error dialog in JavaScript. We don't need to do anything if it's a normal request because the page will be reloaded and the form will display any errors in the input.

```
  if ajax:
    return render_to_response(
      'bookmark_save_form.html', variables
    )
  else:
    return render_to_response('bookmark_save.html', variables)
```

This check is done at the end of the method. The execution reaches this point if there is no POST data, which means that we should render a form and return it. We use the `bookmark_save_form.html` template if it's an AJAX request, or `bookmark_save.html` otherwise.

Our view is now ready to serve AJAX requests as well as normal page requests. Let's write the JavaScript code that will take advantage of the updated view. Create a new file called `bookmark_edit.js` in `site_media`. But before we add any code to it, let's link `bookmark_edit.js` to the `user_page.html` template. Open the `user_page.html` template and modify it as follows:

```
{% extends "base.html" %}
  {% block external %}
    <script type="text/javascript"
      src="/site_media/bookmark_edit.js">
    </script>
  {% endblock %}
{% block title %}{{ username }}{% endblock %}
{% block head %}Bookmarks for {{ username }}{% endblock %}
{% block content %}
{% include "bookmark_list.html" %}
{% endblock %}
```

We have to write two functions in the `bookmark_edit.js` file:

- `bookmark_edit`: The function handles clicks on edit links. It loads an edit form from the server, and replaces the bookmark with this form.

- `bookmark_save`: The function handles the submissions of edit forms, sends form data to the server, and replaces the form with the bookmark HTML returned by the server.

Let's start with the first function. Open the `site_media/bookmark_edit.js` file and write the following code in it:

```
function bookmark_edit() {
  var item = $(this).parent();
  var url = item.find(".title").attr("href");
  item.load(
    "/save/?ajax&url=" + encodeURIComponent(url),
```

```
        null,
        function () {
          $("#save-form").submit(bookmark_save);
        }
    );
    return false;
}
```

As this function handles click events on an edit link, the variable `this` refers to the edit link. Wrapping it in the jQuery `$()` function and calling `parent()` returns the parent of the edit link, which is the `<li>` element of the bookmark (try it in the Firebug console to see for yourself).

After retrieving a reference to the bookmark's `<li>` element, we obtain a reference to the bookmark's title and extract the bookmark's URL from it using the `attr()` method.

Next, we use the `load()` method to put an editing form in place of the bookmark's HTML. This time we are calling `load()` with two extra arguments in addition to the URL. `load()` takes two optional parameters:

- An object of key/value pairs, if we are sending a POST request: Since we get the edit form from the server-side view using a GET request, we pass `null` for this parameter.
- A function that is called when jQuery finishes loading the URL into the selected element: The function we are passing attaches `bookmark_save` (which we are going to write next) to the form that we've just retrieved.

Finally, the function returns `false` to tell the browser not to follow the edit link.

Now we need to attach the `bookmark_edit` function to the event of clicking an edit link using `$(document).ready()`:

```
$(document).ready(function () {
  $("ul.bookmarks .edit").click(bookmark_edit);
});
```

If you try to edit a bookmark in the user page after writing this function, an edit form should appear. But you should also get a JavaScript error message in the Firebug console because the function `bookmark_save` is not defined, so let's write it:

```
function bookmark_save() {
  var item = $(this).parent();
  var data = {
    url: item.find("#id_url").val(),
    title: item.find("#id_title").val(),
```

```
      tags: item.find("#id_tags").val()
   };
   $.post("/save/?ajax", data, function (result) {
     if (result != "failure") {
       item.before($("li", result).get(0));
       item.remove();
       $("ul.bookmarks .edit").click(bookmark_edit);
     }
     else {
       alert("Failed to validate bookmark before saving.");
     }
   });
   return false;
}
```

Here, the variable `this` refers to the edit form because we are handling the event of submitting a form. The function starts by retrieving a reference to the form's parent, which is again the bookmark's `<li>` element. Next, the function retrieves the updated data from the form using the ID of each form field and the `val()` method. Then it uses a method called `$.post()` to send the data back to the server. Finally, it returns `false` to prevent the browser from submitting the form.

As you may have guessed, `$.post()` is a jQuery method that sends POST requests to the server. It takes three parameters:

- The URL of the target of the POST request.
- An object of key/value pairs that represent POST data.
- A function that is invoked when the request is done. Server response is passed to this function as a string parameter.

It's worth mentioning that jQuery provides a method called `$.get()` for sending a GET request to the server. It takes the same types of parameters as `$.post()`.

We use `$.post()` to send the updated bookmark data to the `bookmark_save_page` view. As discussed a few paragraphs ago, the view returns the updated bookmark HTML if it succeeds in saving it. Otherwise, it returns the string `"failure"`. Therefore, we check whether the result returned from the server is `"failure"` or not. If the request succeeds, we insert the new bookmark before the old one using the `before()` method and remove the old bookmark from the HTML document using `remove()`. If, on the other hand, the request fails, we display an alert box saying so.

Several little things remain before we finish this section: Why do we insert `$("li", result).get(0)` instead of `result`? If you check the `bookmark_save_page` view, you will see that it uses the `bookmark_list.html` template to construct the bookmark's HTML. However, the `bookmark_list.html` template returns the bookmark `<li>` element wrapped in a `<ul>` tag. Basically, `$("li", result).get(0)` tells jQuery to extract the first `<li>` element in `result`, and this is the element that we want. As you see from this snippet, you can use the jQuery `$()` function to select elements from an HTML string by passing this string as a second argument to the function.

`bookmark_submit` is attached to its event from within `bookmark_edit`, so we don't need to do anything about it in `$(document).ready()`.

Lastly, after loading the updated bookmark into the page, we call `$("ul.bookmarks .edit").click(bookmark_edit)` again to attach `bookmark_edit` to the newly-loaded edit link. If you don't do so and try to edit a bookmark twice, the second click on the edit link will take you to a separate form page.

When you have finished writing the JavaScript code, open your browser and go to your user page to experiment with the new feature. Edit the bookmarks, save them, and notice how the changes are immediately reflected on the page without any reloading:

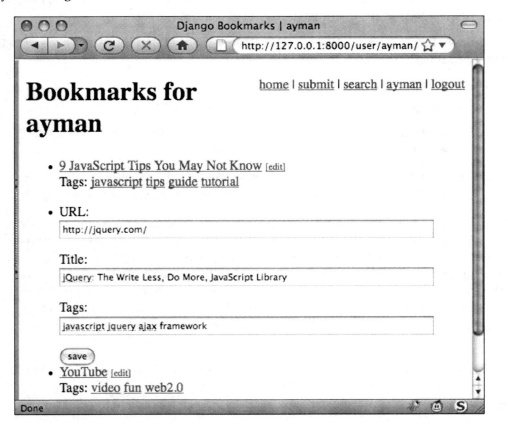

Now that you have completed this section, you should have a good understanding of how in-place editing is implemented. There are many other scenarios where this feature can be useful. For example, it can be used to edit an article or a comment on the same page without navigating away to a form located on a different URL.

In the next section we will implement a third common AJAX feature that helps the user enter tags when submitting a bookmark.

Auto-completion of tags

The last AJAX enhancement that we are going to implement in this chapter is auto-completion of tags. The concept of auto-completion found its way into web applications when Google released their **Suggest** searching interface. Suggest works by displaying the most popular search queries below the search input field based on what the user has typed so far. It's also similar to how code editors in integrated development environments offer code-completion suggestions based on what you type. This feature saves time by letting the user type a few characters of the word they want and then select it from a list, without having to type it completely.

We will implement this feature by offering suggestions when the user enters tags while submitting a bookmark. But instead of writing this feature from scratch, we are going to use a jQuery plug-in to implement it. jQuery enjoys a large and continually growing list of plug-ins that provide a variety of features. Installing a plug-in is no different from installing jQuery itself. You download one or more files and link them to your template, and then write a few lines of JavaScript code to activate the plug-in.

You can browse the list of available jQuery plug-ins by pointing your browser to `http://docs.jquery.com/Plugins`. Search for the auto-complete plug-in in the list, and download it. Or you can directly grab it from the following URL:

`http://bassistance.de/jquery-plugins/jquery-plugin-autocomplete/`

You will get a ZIP archive with many files in it. Extract the following files to the `site_media` directory:

- `jquery.autocomplete.css`
- `dimensions.js`
- `jquery.bgiframe.min.js`
- `jquery.autocomplete.js`

Since we want to offer the autocomplete feature on the bookmark submission page, create an empty file called `tag_autocomplete.js` in the `site_media` directory. Then open the `templates/bookmark_save.html` template and link all of the files in the bulleted list on the previous page to it:

```
{% extends "base.html" %}
{% block external %}
  <link rel="stylesheet"
    href="/site_media/jquery.autocomplete.css"
    type="text/css" />
  <script type="text/javascript"
    src="/site_media/dimensions.js"></script>
  <script type="text/javascript"
    src="/site_media/jquery.bgiframe.min.js"></script>
  <script type="text/javascript"
    src="/site_media/jquery.autocomplete.js"></script>
  <script type="text/javascript"
    src="/site_media/tag_autocomplete.js"></script>
{% endblock %}
{% block title %}Save Bookmark{% endblock %}
{% block head %}Save Bookmark{% endblock %}
[...]
```

We have now finished installing the plug-in. If you read its documentation, you will find that this plug-in is activated by calling a method named `autocomplete()` on a selected input element. `autocomplete()` takes the following parameters:

- A server-side URL: The plug-in sends a GET request to this URL with what has been typed so far, and expects the server to return a set of suggestions.

- An object that can be used to specify various options: Ones that are of interest to us are `multiple` and `multipleSeparator`. `multiple` is a Boolean variable that tells the plug-in that the input field is used to enter multiple values (remembering that we use the same text field to enter all tags). `multipleSeparator` is used to tell the plug-in which string separates multiple entries. In our case, it's a single space character.

So before activating the plug-in, we need to write a view that receives user input and returns a set of suggestions. Open the `bookmarks/views.py` file and append the following to its end:

```
def ajax_tag_autocomplete(request):
    if 'q' in request.GET:
        tags = Tag.objects.filter(
            name__istartswith=request.GET['q']
        )[:10]
        return HttpResponse(u'\n'.join(tag.name for tag in tags))
    return HttpResponse()
```

The `autocomplete` plug-in sends user input in a `GET` variable named `q`. Therefore, we check that this variable exists, and builds a list of tags whose names begin with the value of this variable. This is done using the `filter` method and the `istartswith` operator that we learned about earlier this chapter. We only take the first 10 results to avoid overwhelming the user with suggestions, and also to reduce bandwidth and performance costs. Finally, we join the suggestions into a single string separated by newlines, wrap the string into an `HttpResponse` object, and return it.

With the suggestion view ready, create a URL entry to it in the `urls.py` file:

```
urlpatterns = patterns('',
    [...]
    # Ajax
    (r'^ajax/tag/autocomplete/$', ajax_tag_autocomplete),
)
```

Now, activate the plug-in on the tags input field by entering the following code into `site_media/tag_autocomplete.js`:

```
$(document).ready(function () {
    $("#id_tags").autocomplete(
        '/ajax/tag/autocomplete/',
        {multiple: true, multipleSeparator: ' '}
    );
});
```

The code passed an anonymous function to `$(document).ready()`. This function invokes `autocomplete()` on the tags input field, passing the arguments that we talked about earlier.

These few lines of code are all that we need in order to implement auto-completion of the tags. To test the new feature, navigate to the bookmark submission form at `http://127.0.0.1:8000/save/` and try to enter a character or two into the tags field. Suggestions should appear based on the tags available in your database.

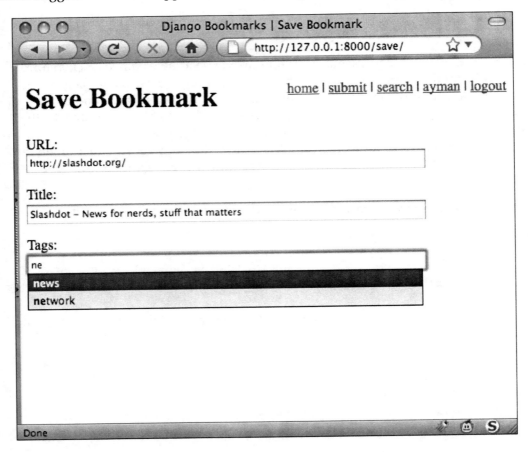

With this feature we finish the chapter. We have covered a lot of material and have learned about many exciting technologies and techniques. After reading the chapter, you should be able to think of and implement many other enhancements to the user interface, such as the ability to delete bookmarks from the user page or to do live browsing of the bookmarks by tags, and so on.

The next chapter will shift to a different topic. We will let users vote and comment on their favorite bookmarks and the front page of our application won't remain as empty as it is now.

Summary

Phew! This was a long chapter, but hopefully you have learned a lot from it. We started the chapter with learning about the jQuery framework and how to integrate it into our Django project. After that, we implemented three exciting features into our bookmarking application: live searching, in-place editing, and auto-completion.

The next chapter is going to be equally exciting. We will let users submit bookmarks to the front page and vote for their favorite bookmarks. We will also enable users to comment on bookmarks. So keep reading!

7
Voting and Commenting

The main idea behind our application is to provide easy ways for users to discover and share bookmarks. One way to achieve this is to allow users to recommend bookmarks to each other. Since the main page of our application is empty, apart from a welcome message, we will enable users to share bookmarks with other users by submitting their favorite bookmarks to the main page of the application. After that, we will let other users vote for the bookmarks that they like, and then create a page for the most popular bookmarks by votes. This set of features will provide a fresh list of interesting bookmarks selected by our community of users. In the second part of this chapter, we will enable commenting on bookmarks. It will let users share opinions and discuss the bookmarks that are posted on our site. This chapter brings many exciting features to our application, and you will learn several new Django features while working through it.

In this chapter, you will learn how to:

- Let users share their bookmarks on the main page
- Enable users to vote for their favorite bookmarks
- Display the recently shared and the most popular bookmarks
- Enable users to comment on bookmarks

Sharing bookmarks on the main page

So far, our users are able to discover new bookmarks by browsing tag and user pages. Let's provide a new method for users to share and discover new bookmarks. When saving a bookmark, we will give users the option of sharing this bookmark on the main page of our application. When a bookmark is shared, other users will be able to vote for the bookmark if they like it. We will also create a page where users can see the popular bookmarks by votes. This feature is important for our application because it will change the main page from a basic welcome page to a frequently updated list of bookmarks, where users will be able to find new and interesting content.

Our strategy for implementing this feature consists of the following steps:

1. Create a data model for storing bookmarks that are shared on the main page. This model will keep a track of various pieces of information related to the shared bookmark.

2. Modify the bookmark submission form so that it enables users to share their bookmarks on the main page.

3. Change the main page so that it displays the recently shared bookmarks. Each bookmark will have a vote button next to its title.

4. Create a view that receives voting requests from users and updates vote counts.

This feature carries a considerable amount of work, but the results will be worth it, and we will learn a lot of useful information during the process. Let's get started!

The SharedBookmark data model

When a bookmark is shared on the main page, we need to store the following information in the database:

- The date on which the bookmark was shared: We need this in order to display popular bookmarks over a certain period of time

- The number of votes for this bookmark

- The users who voted for this bookmark: This is needed to prevent users from voting for the same bookmark twice

For this purpose, we will create a new data model called `SharedBookmark`. Open the `bookmarks/models.py` file and add the following class to it:

```
class SharedBookmark(models.Model):
    bookmark = models.ForeignKey(Bookmark, unique=True)
    date = models.DateTimeField(auto_now_add=True)
    votes = models.IntegerField(default=1)
    users_voted = models.ManyToManyField(User)

    def __unicode__(self):
      return u'%s, %s' % (self.bookmark, self.votes)
```

This data model utilizes features that we haven't used before, so we will go through its fields one by one:

- The `bookmark` field is a foreign key that refers back to the bookmark that is being shared. We want it to be unique so that the same bookmark cannot be shared more than once.

- The `date` field is of the type `models.DateTimeField`. As its name suggests, you can use this field to store a date/time value. The argument `auto_now_add` tells Django to automatically set this field to the current date/time when an object of this data model is first created.

- The `votes` field is of the type `models.IntegerField`. This field holds an integer value. By using `default=1` with this field, we tell Django to set the field's value to 1 when an object of this data model is first created.

- The `users_voted` many-to-many field contains the list of users who voted for this shared bookmark.

After entering the data model code into the `bookmarks/models.py` file, run the following command to create its corresponding tables in the database:

```
$ python manage.py syncdb
```

With this, we can store all the information that we need to maintain shared bookmarks. Next, we are going to enable users to share bookmarks on the main page.

Modifying the bookmark submission form

We will let users share bookmarks on the main page by providing a checkbox on the bookmark submission form. If the user enables this checkbox, the bookmark is shared. To implement this, we first need to modify the class that represents the bookmark submission form. So, open the `bookmarks/forms.py` file and modify the `BookmarkSaveForm` class as follows:

```
class BookmarkSaveForm(forms.Form):
  url = forms.URLField(
    label='URL',
    widget=forms.TextInput(attrs={'size': 64})
  )
  title = forms.CharField(
    label='Title',
    widget=forms.TextInput(attrs={'size': 64})
  )
  tags = forms.CharField(
    label='Tags',
    required=False,
    widget=forms.TextInput(attrs={'size': 64})
  )
  share = forms.BooleanField(
    label=u'Share on the main page',
    required=False
  )
```

We have added a new field of the type `forms.BooleanField` to BookmarkSaveForm. This field can either be `True` or `False`, and it is rendered as a checkbox when the form is displayed.

Next, we will modify the method that saves bookmarks so that it takes the new checkbox into account. Open the `bookmarks/views.py` file and add the highlighted lines to the _save_bookmark method:

```
def _bookmark_save(request, form):
  # Create or get link.
  link, dummy = Link.objects.get_or_create(
    url=form.clean_data['url']
  )
  # Create or get bookmark.
  bookmark, created = Bookmark.objects.get_or_create(
    user=request.user,
    link=link
  )
  # Update bookmark title.
  bookmark.title = form.clean_data['title']
  # If the bookmark is being updated, clear old tag list.
  if not created:
    bookmark.tag_set.clear()
  # Create new tag list.
  tag_names = form.clean_data['tags'].split()
  for tag_name in tag_names:
    tag, dummy = Tag.objects.get_or_create(name=tag_name)
    bookmark.tag_set.add(tag)
  # Share on the main page if requested.
  if form.cleaned_data['share']:
    shared, created = SharedBookmark.objects.get_or_create(
      bookmark=bookmark
    )
    if created:
      shared.users_voted.add(request.user)
      shared.save()
  # Save bookmark to database and return it.
  bookmark.save()
  return bookmark
```

The new code works like this. If the Share checkbox was enabled in the bookmark submission form, we use get_or_create to check whether a SharedBookmark object exists for the bookmark or create one if nothing exists. If the SharedBookmark object is created by get_or_create, we add the current user to the list of users who voted for the bookmark, and save the SharedBookmark object. Notice that we don't need to do anything if the Share checkbox is not enabled, or if a SharedBookmark object already exists for the current bookmark.

This is all that we need to do in order to let users share bookmarks on the main page. At this stage, if a user enables the `Share` checkbox when saving a bookmark, a `SharedBookmark` object with the corresponding data is created. So in the next subsection, we will display a list of the recently shared bookmarks on the main page and let users vote for their favorite bookmarks.

Browsing and voting for shared bookmarks

Now we have a data model that stores all bookmarks that were shared by users. It should be pretty easy to get a list of the most recent bookmarks from this data model and display it on the main page. First, modify the `main_page` view in the `bookmarks/views.py` file to retrieve this list and pass it to the template.

```
def main_page(request):
    shared_bookmarks = SharedBookmark.objects.order_by(
        '-date'
    )[:10]
    variables = RequestContext(request, {
        'shared_bookmarks': shared_bookmarks
    })
    return render_to_response('main_page.html', variables)
```

The new code for the view is straightforward. We call the `order_by` method on `SharedBookmark.objects` to retrieve a list of shared bookmarks ordered by date in a descending order (notice the minus sign in `'-date'`), and then use the slice syntax to limit the list of shared bookmarks to the first 10 results. After that, we put the list in a `RequestContext` and pass it to the `main_page.html` template.

Next, we need to modify the main page so that it displays the list of shared bookmarks. We usually use the `bookmark_list.html` template to display bookmark lists. However, here we have a list of `SharedBookmark` objects and not ordinary `Bookmark` objects. Therefore, we will write a separate template that will render lists of shared bookmarks. The output of this template will be slightly different from `bookmark_list.html`. For example, it will display the vote count for each bookmark. Create a new file called `shared_bookmark_list.html` in the templates directory and put the following code in it:

```
{% if shared_bookmarks %}
  <ul class="bookmarks">
    {% for shared_bookmark in shared_bookmarks %}
      <li>
        <a href="{{ shared_bookmark.bookmark.link.url }}"
          class="title">
          {{ shared_bookmark.bookmark.title }}</a>
        <br />
```

```
            Posted By:
<a href="/user/{{ shared_bookmark.bookmark.user.username }}/"
            class="username">
            {{ shared_bookmark.bookmark.user.username }}</a> |
        <span class="vote-count">Votes:
            {{ shared_bookmark.votes }}</span>
      </li>
    {% endfor %}
  </ul>
{% else %}
  <p>No bookmarks found.</p>
{% endif %}
```

The outline of this template is similar to `bookmark_list.html` so it should be easy to understand. First, the template checks the list of shared bookmarks to see if it's empty or not. Then it iterates through the shared bookmarks and prints a link for each bookmark along with some information about it, such as the user who posted the bookmark and the number of votes for the bookmark.

After creating the `shared_bookmark_list.html` template, we need to include it in the template of the main page. Open the `main_page.html` template and insert the highlighted line into it:

```
{% extends "base.html" %}

{% block title %}Welcome to Django Bookmarks{% endblock %}
{% block head %}Welcome to Django Bookmarks{% endblock %}

{% block content %}
  {% if user.username %}
    <p>Welcome {{ user.username }}!
      Here you can store and share bookmarks!</p>
  {% else %}
    <p>Welcome anonymous user!
      You need to <a href="/login/">login</a>
      before you can store and share bookmarks.</p>
  {% endif %}
  <h2>Bookmarks Shared by Users</h2>
  {% include "shared_bookmark_list.html" %}
{% endblock %}
```

You can try out the new main page by running the development server (if you haven't done so already) and sharing a couple of bookmarks using the bookmark submission form, and then opening the main page at `http://127.0.0.1:8000/`. The output should be similar to the following:

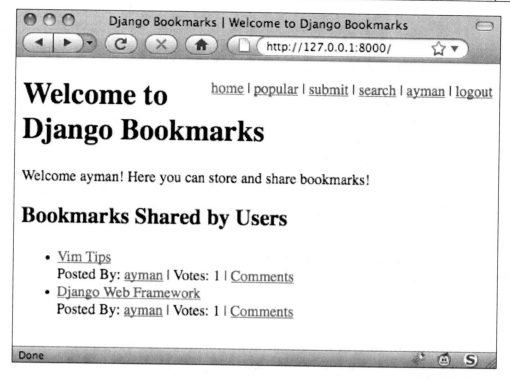

We are almost there! The shared bookmark now appears on the main page, but its vote count is set to one, and you have no way to vote. So we will fix this next.

Let's create a view that receives voting requests for a shared bookmark and increments the vote count for the bookmark. If you remember from a previous chapter, when you write a data model, Django automatically adds an attribute called id to this data model. This attribute is a unique integer that can be used to identify the object. We will use this attribute to identify votes for shared bookmarks.

Let's start by writing the view function. Open the bookmarks/views.py file and add the following code to it:

```
@login_required
def bookmark_vote_page(request):
    if 'id' in request.GET:
        try:
            id = request.GET['id']
            shared_bookmark = SharedBookmark.objects.get(id=id)
            user_voted = shared_bookmark.users_voted.filter(
                username=request.user.username
            )
```

```
    if not user_voted:
        shared_bookmark.votes += 1
        shared_bookmark.users_voted.add(request.user)
        shared_bookmark.save()
except SharedBookmark.DoesNotExist:
    raise Http404('Bookmark not found.')

if 'HTTP_REFERER' in request.META:
    return HttpResponseRedirect(request.META['HTTP_REFERER'])
return HttpResponseRedirect('/')
```

Let's see how this view works by going through each section of the code:

```
@login_required
def bookmark_vote_page(request):
```

We apply the `login_required` decorator to the view because only logged-in users should be able to vote.

```
if 'id' in request.GET:
    try:
        id = request.GET['id']
        shared_bookmark = SharedBookmark.objects.get(id=id)
```

The view starts by looking for a GET variable called `id`. If it finds one, it retrieves the `SharedBookmark` object that is associated with this `id`.

```
user_voted = shared_bookmark.users_voted.filter(
    username=request.user.username
)
```

Next, the view checks to see whether the user has voted for this bookmark before. This is done by calling the `filter` method on the `shared_bookmark.users_voted` attribute and passing the `username` to it. If the user has not voted before, the filter will return an empty result:

```
if not user_voted:
    shared_bookmark.votes += 1
    shared_bookmark.users_voted.add(request.user)
    shared_bookmark.save()
```

If this is the first time that the user has voted for this bookmark, we increment the `shared_bookmark.votes` attribute by one, add the current user to the `shared_bookmark.users_voted` attribute, and save the `shared_bookmark` object.

```
except SharedBookmark.DoesNotExist:
    raise Http404('Bookmark not found.')
```

If `id` does not map to a shared bookmark object, we raise an `Ttp404` exception, which generates a 404 page not found error.

```
If 'HTTP_REFERER' in request.META:
    return HttpResponseRedirect(request.META['HTTP_REFERER'])
return HttpResponseRedirect('/')
```

Finally, if everything goes well, we redirect users to the page they came from. This is done by using an HTTP header called `HTTP_REFERER`. When you click a link, your browser sends the URL of the page that contains the link to the web server that hosts the target of the link. Here, we take advantage of this feature to redirect back from the vote view to the page that the user came from. This is necessary if we want to display vote links on pages other than the main page, as we will do later in this chapter.

HTTP headers are available to Django views at `request.META`. Some browsers do not send the `HTTP_REFERER` header. We first check to make sure that this header exists. If it does not exist, we redirect to the main page.

Next, we will add a URL entry for the vote view. Open the `urls.py` file and add the highlighted line to `urlpatterns`:

```
urlpatterns = patterns('',
    [...]
    # Account management
    (r'^save/$', bookmark_save_page),
    (r'^vote/$', bookmark_vote_page),
)
```

The new URL entry should be easy to understand by now. We are mapping the URL `^vote/$` to a method called `bookmark_vote_page`.

The vote view is ready. Now we only need to create links for it in the main page. So open the `shared_bookmark_list.html` template and add the highlighted code line to it:

```
{% if shared_bookmarks %}
  <ul class="bookmarks">
    {% for shared_bookmark in shared_bookmarks %}
      <li>
        <a href="/vote/?id={{ shared_bookmark.id }}"
           class="vote">[+]</a>
        <a href="{{ shared_bookmark.bookmark.link.url }}"
           class="title">
          {{ shared_bookmark.bookmark.title }}</a>
        <br />
```

```
      Posted By:
<a href="/user/{{ shared_bookmark.bookmark.user.username }}/"
         class="username">
         {{ shared_bookmark.bookmark.user.username }}</a> |
      <span class="vote-count">Votes:
            {{ shared_bookmark.votes }}</span>
    </li>
  {% endfor %}
 </ul>
{% else %}
 <p>No bookmarks found.</p>
{% endif %}
```

The highlighted line adds a link to the vote view with the text `[+]`. The URL of the link is generated by appending `shared_bookmark.id` to `/vote/?id=`.

With this, we finish implementing the voting feature. If you refresh the main page now, you should see a page similar to the following screenshot:

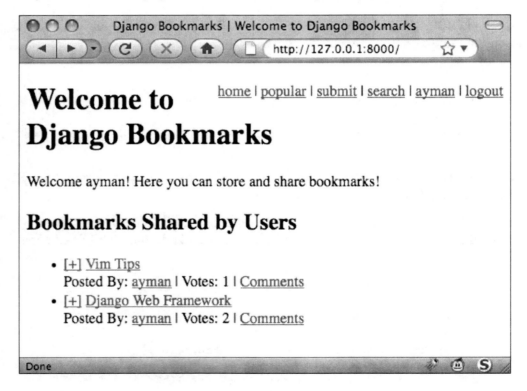

If you try to click one of the vote buttons, the vote may or may not increase, depending on whether you are the creator of the bookmark. Remember that if you share a bookmark, you are automatically considered to have voted for it. Therefore, it is a good idea to register multiple accounts and try to vote using these accounts.

The main page now displays the 10 most recent bookmarks that were shared by users. But what if we want to see the most popular bookmarks according to vote counts? The next subsection creates a page that provides this feature.

The popular bookmarks page

We can easily implement a popular bookmarks page in a way similar to the main page. We simply need to sort by votes instead of date. However, in order to keep the popular page fresh every day, we will make it display the most popular bookmarks that were submitted on the last day only.

The first step when implementing the popular bookmarks page is to create a view. So open the `bookmarks/views.py` file and add the following method to it:

```
from datetime import datetime, timedelta

def popular_page(request):
  today = datetime.today()
  yesterday = today - timedelta(1)

  shared_bookmarks = SharedBookmark.objects.filter(
    date__gt=yesterday
  )
  shared_bookmarks = shared_bookmarks.order_by(
    '-votes'
  )[:10]
  variables = RequestContext(request, {
    'shared_bookmarks': shared_bookmarks
  })
  return render_to_response('popular_page.html', variables)
```

This view is a little more involved than the `main_page` view. The tricky part is obtaining the date/time of yesterday and retrieving the list of shared bookmarks according to it. Let's go through each section of the code:

```
from datetime import datetime, timedelta

def popular_page(request):
  today = datetime.today()
  yesterday = today - timedelta(1)
```

We import the `datetime` and `timedelta` classes from the `datetime` module. The `datetime` module is a standard Python module, and it is very useful for manipulating dates and times. A `datetime` object represents a particular date and time, whereas a `timedelta` object represents duration or the difference between two times.

In the `popular_page` view, we use the `datetime.today` method to get a `datetime` object that represents today. Next, we create a `timedelta` object that represents a single day and then subtract this object from `today` to get the date/time of yesterday.

```
shared_bookmarks = SharedBookmark.objects.filter(
    date__gt=yesterday
)
shared_bookmarks = shared_bookmarks.order_by(
    '-votes'
)[:10]
```

Here, we first apply `filter` on `SharedBookmark.objects` to obtain all the shared bookmarks that were submitted after the value of `yesterday`. This is done by passing the argument `date__gt=yesterday` to `filter` (`__gt` here stands for greater than). Passing `date__gt=yesterday` to `filter` retrieves all the bookmarks whose `date` is greater than `yesterday`.

Next, we call `order_by` on the result from the previous call to sort it by the number of votes in descending order. We used the slice syntax to limit the number of bookmarks to 10:

```
variables = RequestContext(request, {
    'shared_bookmarks': shared_bookmarks
})
return render_to_response('popular_page.html', variables)
```

Finally, we pass the `shared_bookmarks` list to a template called `popular_page.html` to render the page.

Now let's write the template for the popular page. Create a new file called `popular_page.html` in the templates directory and put the following code into it:

```
{% extends "base.html" %}
{% block title %}Popular Bookmarks{% endblock %}
{% block head %}Popular Bookmarks{% endblock %}
{% block content %}
  {% include "shared_bookmark_list.html" %}
{% endblock %}
```

The template is pretty straightforward. It simply defines blocks from the `base.html` file and includes the `shared_bookmark_list.html` file.

Lastly, we need a URL entry for the new view, so open the `urls.py` file and add the highlighted code line to `urlpatterns`:

```
urlpatterns = patterns('',
    # Browsing
    (r'^$', main_page),
    (r'^popular/$', popular_page),
    (r'^user/(\w+)/$', user_page),
    (r'^tag/([^\s]+)/$', tag_page),
    (r'^tag/$', tag_cloud_page),
    (r'^search/$', search_page),
    [...]
)
```

And that's it. Navigate to `http://127.0.0.1:8000/popular/` to see the popular bookmarks page. Notice how bookmarks are ordered by vote count on this page. If you try to vote for a bookmark, you will be redirected back to the same page. Feel free to add a link to this page in the navigation menu by editing the `templates/base.html` file and adding the highlighted code line from the following code snippet:

```
[...]
    <div id="nav">
        <a href="/">home</a> |
        <a href="/popular/">popular</a> |
        {% if user.is_authenticated %}
            <a href="/save/">submit</a> |
            <a href="/search/">search</a> |
            <a href="/user/{{ user.username }}/">
                {{ user.username }}</a> |
            <a href="/logout/">logout</a>
        {% else %}
            <a href="/login/">login</a> |
            <a href="/register/">register</a>
        {% endif %}
    </div>
[...]
```

This section wasn't difficult was it? The features needed some effort to be implemented, but there weren't any major hurdles. Now, the users of our application are able to share and vote for their favorite bookmarks, and browse a daily list of popular bookmarks. The next section brings another exciting feature to our application. We will let users post comments on shared bookmarks.

Commenting on bookmarks

Voting on bookmarks is one way for our users to express their opinions. How about giving users more flexibility in expressing opinions by letting them comment on bookmarks? Comments will be an excellent method for users to discuss their interests amongst each other and make new friends. In this section, we will implement the commenting feature in our application.

The process of adding comments to a Django application consists of the following steps:

- Enable the comments application and create its models in the database
- Use a set of template tags provided by the comments application to display a comment form and a list of comments on a page
- Create templates for the comment submission form and the page that appears after successfully posting a comment

Django makes implementing a complex feature, such as commenting, extremely easy, as you will see. After going through this section, you will be able to add comments to any Django application with ease.

Enabling the comments application

The comments application that comes with Django lives in `django.contrib.comments`. Like any other Django application, enabling comments requires a few simple steps. First, edit the `settings.py` file and add `'django.contrib.comments'` to the `INSTALLED_APPS` variables:

```
INSTALLED_APPS = (
   'django.contrib.auth',
   'django.contrib.contenttypes',
   'django.contrib.sessions',
   'django.contrib.sites',
   'django.contrib.comments',
   'django_bookmarks.bookmarks'
)
```

Second, run the following command to create tables for the data models of the comments application in the database:

```
$ python manage.py syncdb
```

After that, we need to add URL entries for the views that are provided by the comments application. Since the comments application contains many views, it would be a tedious and repetitive task to add a URL entry for each one manually. Django provides a shortcut for this. The comments application defines all of its URL entries in a module located at `django.contrib.comments.urls`, and we can include these entries in our project under a particular path by using a function called `include`. Open the `urls.py` file and add the following highlighted lines to it:

```
urlpatterns = patterns('',
  [...]
  # Comments
  (r'^comments/',
    include('django.contrib.comments.urls')),
)
```

This looks different from how we usually define URL entries. We are basically telling Django to retrieve all the URL entries in the `django.contrib.comments.urls` module and include them in our application under the path `^comment/`. This will make the views of the comments application accessible from within our project.

With this, we have finished. The comments application is now ready to be used.

Creating a view for comments

Since we want users to be able to comment on shared bookmarks, we need a separate page for each shared bookmark where comments are displayed. We will create a new view for this purpose. This view will receive the ID of the shared bookmark in the URL, and display the shared bookmark, its comments, and a form for posting new comments.

Let's start by defining a URL entry for this view. Open the `urls.py` file and add the highlighted line of code to the `urlpatterns` object:

```
urlpatterns = patterns('',
  # Browsing
  (r'^$', main_page),
  (r'^popular/$', popular_page),
  (r'^user/(\w+)/$', user_page),
  (r'^tag/([^\s]+)/$', tag_page),
  (r'^tag/$', tag_cloud_page),
  (r'^search/$', search_page),
  (r'^bookmark/(\d+)/$', bookmark_page),
  [...]
)
```

The new URL entry for the bookmark page looks similar to the URL entry of the user page. However, the regular expression for the `bookmark_page` view uses the sequence \d instead of \w. If you recall from Chapter 3, \w means any alphanumeric character. You may have guessed that \d here means any decimal digit. This is because the `bookmark_page` view takes a bookmark ID in the URL, and the bookmark IDs consist of decimal digits only. Also, you may remember that putting parentheses around a part of the regular expression captures the string matched by this part and passes it to the view as an additional parameter.

Now, let's write the `bookmark_page` view. Open the `bookmarks/views.py` file and add the following method to it:

```
def bookmark_page(request, bookmark_id):
    shared_bookmark = get_object_or_404(
        SharedBookmark,
        id=bookmark_id
    )
    variables = RequestContext(request, {
        'shared_bookmark': shared_bookmark
    })
    return render_to_response('bookmark_page.html', variables)
```

This view is pretty straightforward. It uses `get_object_or_404` to retrieve the `SharedBookmark` object associated with the bookmark ID in the URL. After that, it passes the object to a template called `bookmark_page.html`.

Lastly, we need to create the template of the `bookmark_page` view. Create a new file called `bookmark_page.html` in the `templates` directory and insert the following code into it:

```
{% extends "base.html" %}
{% block title %}Bookmark:
    {{ shared_bookmark.bookmark.title }}{% endblock %}
{% block head %}
  <a href="/vote/?id={{ shared_bookmark.id }}"
     class="vote">[+]</a>
  <a href="{{ shared_bookmark.bookmark.link.url }}"
     class="title">
  {{ shared_bookmark.bookmark.title }}</a>
{% endblock %}
{% block content %}
  Posted By:
<a href="/user/{{ shared_bookmark.bookmark.user.username }}/"
     class="username">
    {{ shared_bookmark.bookmark.user.username }}</a> |
  <span class="vote-count">Votes: {{ shared_bookmark.votes }}</span>
{% endblock %}
```

Again, there is nothing special in this template. We display the bookmark and a vote link next to it in the head section, and some information about the bookmark in the content section.

Creating the `bookmark_page` view was a simple task, but next comes the exciting part. We will add a list of comments and a comment form to this view.

Displaying comments and a comment form

The comments application that comes with Django makes it astonishingly easy to add comments to your application. Basically, the comments application provides the following three template tags for you to use in your template:

- `get_comment_count`: It returns the number of comments for the current page
- `get_comment_list`: It returns the list of comments for the current page
- `render_comment_form`: It displays a comment form that can be used to post comments

These tags are not available in templates by default. To activate them, you need to put the following line at the beginning of your template:

```
{% load comments %}
```

The `load` tag is usually used to enable additional template tags that are not available by default.

Each one of these tags takes the following parameters:

- The content type of the object that is receiving comments. The following format should be used for the parameter: `application.model` (all in lowercase).
- The ID of the object that is receiving comments.

So if you want to get the number of comments for a shared bookmark, use the following in the `bookmark_page.html` file:

```
{% get_comment_count for bookmarks.sharedbookmark
     shared_bookmark.id as comment_count %}
```

Now the template variable `comment_count` contains the number of comments for the current shared bookmark.

Similarly, to get the list of comments for a shared bookmark, use the following code in the `bookmark_page.html` file:

```
{% get_comment_list for bookmarks.sharedbookmark
     shared_bookmark.id as comment_list %}
```

Now the template variable `comment_list` contains the list of comments for the current shared bookmark. Each comment in the list provides the following attributes:

- `user`: The `User` object of the user who posted the comment
- `submit_date`: The date/time on which the comment was submitted
- `comment`: The actual comment text
- `ip_address`: The IP address from which the comment was posted

Finally, if you want to display a comment form for a shared bookmark, use the following in the `bookmark_page.html` template:

```
{% render_comment_form for bookmarks.sharedbookmark
   shared_bookmark.id %}
```

 Be careful when typing these template tags, as the whole tag must be on the same line for Django to parse it correctly.

Let's put all of the above information to use. Open the `templates/bookmark_page.html` template and add the highlighted lines of code to it:

```
{% extends "base.html" %}
{% load comments %}
{% block title %}Bookmark:
    {{ shared_bookmark.bookmark.title }}{% endblock %}
{% block head %}
  <a href="/vote/?id={{ shared_bookmark.id }}"
    class="vote">[+]</a>
  <a href="{{ shared_bookmark.bookmark.link.url }}" class="title">
  {{ shared_bookmark.bookmark.title }}</a>
{% endblock %}
{% block content %}
  Posted By:
<a href="/user/{{ shared_bookmark.bookmark.user.username }}/"
    class="username">
    {{ shared_bookmark.bookmark.user.username }}</a> |
  <span class="vote-count">Votes: {{ shared_bookmark.votes }}</span>
  <h2>Comments</h2>
```

```
{% get_comment_count for bookmarks.sharedbookmark
   shared_bookmark.id as comment_count %}
{% get_comment_list for bookmarks.sharedbookmark
   shared_bookmark.id as comment_list %}

{% for comment in comment_list %}
  <div class="comment">
    <p><b>{{ comment.user.username }}</b> said:</p>
    {{ comment.comment|escape|urlizetrunc:40|linebreaks }}
  </div>
{% endfor %}
<p>Number of comments: {{ comment_count }}</p>

{% render_comment_form for bookmarks.sharedbookmark
   shared_bookmark.id %}
{% endblock %}
```

The new code simply makes use of the template tags above in order to add a list of comments and a comment form to bookmark pages. The code should be easy to understand after reading the information provided in this subsection. The only exception to this is the following line:

```
{{ comment.comment|urlizetrunc:40|linebreaks }}
```

You may remember that this is the syntax for using template filters. We are applying three template filters to the body of each comment:

- `urlizetrunc:40`: This filter converts URLs in the comment into clickable links. If the length of the URL exceeds 40, the anchor text of the link is truncated to 40.

- `linebreaks`: This filter converts line breaks into `<p>` and `<br />` tags.

We are almost done with implementing the comments feature. What remains now is adding a couple of templates for the comment form and the page that appears after posting a comment. We will also make some minor changes to improve the appearance of the comments.

Creating comment templates

The comments application provides generic templates for the steps of the comment posting workflow such as a comment form and a success page. We can also override this and use our own customized templates. Let's create two templates: one for the comment submission form, and one for the page that appears after successfully posting a comment. These templates should be in a directory called `comments` inside the `templates` directory, so create this directory now.

Let's start with the template for the comment submission form. Create a file called `form.html` in `templates/comments/` and put the following code into it:

```
{% load comments %}
{% if user.is_authenticated %}
  <form action="{% comment_form_target %}" method="POST">
    {% for field in form %}
      {% if field.is_hidden %}
        {{ field }}
      {% endif %}
    {% endfor %}
    <input type="hidden" name="name"
      value="{{ user.username }}" />
    <input type="text" name="honeypot" size="64"
      style="display: none;" />
    <label for="id_comment">Comment</label>
    <textarea id="id_comment" rows="10" cols="40"
      name="comment"></textarea>
    <input type="submit" name="submit" class="submit-post"
      value="Post" />
  </form>
{% else %}
  <p>Please <a href="/login/">log in</a> to post comments.</p>
{% endif %}
```

The template displays an HTML form for posting comments if the user is logged in, and a link to the login page otherwise. The values of the form's action and fields were taken from the documentation of the comments application. Don't concern yourself with them.

Next, we will create a template for the page that appears after successfully posting a comment. So create a new file called `posted.html` in `templates/comments/` and put the following code into it:

```
{% extends "base.html" %}

{% block title %}Comment Posted Successfully{% endblock %}

{% block head %}Comment Posted Successfully{% endblock %}

{% block content %}
  <p>Thank you for contributing.</p>
{% endblock %}
```

We have now finished implementing the comments feature. But before we try it, we need to create links to comment pages. Open the `templates/shared_bookmark_list.html` file and change it to the following highlighted line of code:

```
{% if shared_bookmarks %}
  <ul class="bookmarks">
    {% for shared_bookmark in shared_bookmarks %}
      <li>
        <a href="/vote/?id={{ shared_bookmark.id }}"
           class="vote">[+]</a>
        <a href="{{ shared_bookmark.bookmark.link.url }}"
           class="title">
          {{ shared_bookmark.bookmark.title }}</a>
        <br />
        Posted By:
<a href="/user/{{ shared_bookmark.bookmark.user.username }}/"
           class="username">
          {{ shared_bookmark.bookmark.user.username }}</a> |
        <span class="vote-count">Votes:
          {{ shared_bookmark.votes }}</span> |
        <a href="/bookmark/{{ shared_bookmark.id }}/">
          Comments</a>
      </li>
    {% endfor %}
  </ul>
{% else %}
  <p>No bookmarks found.</p>
{% endif %}
```

Let's add some style to our commenting form and comments. Open the `site_media/style.css` file and append the following lines to it:

```
textarea {
  display: block;
}
.comment {
  margin: 1em;
  padding: 5px;
  border: 1px solid #000;
}
```

We have finished! We can finally test this exciting feature. Go to
`http://127.0.0.1:8000/`, click the **Comments** link on one of the shared
bookmarks, and you will see a comment form below the title of the bookmark,
as shown in the following figure:

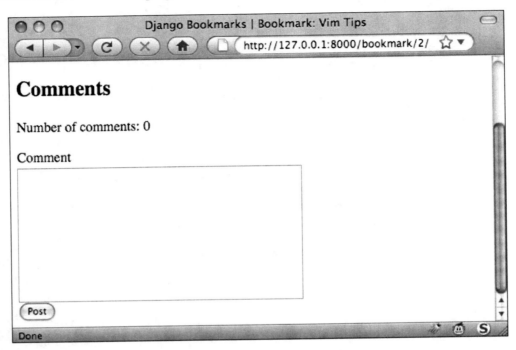

If you try to post a comment, you will get a page that confirms the success of the
operation, as can be seen in the following figure:

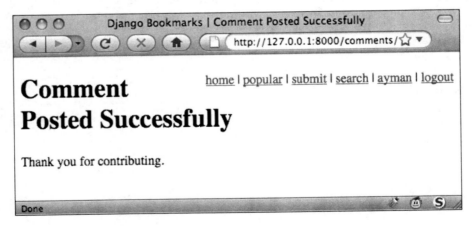

Go back to the bookmarks page to find that your submitted comment now appears before the comment form:

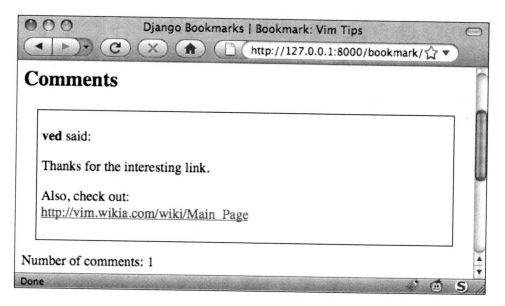

It is amazing that we have gained so much functionality with only a small amount of code. The comments feature took us a minimal amount of work to complete. Most importantly, you are now able to employ the comments applications in your future Django projects.

Summary

In this chapter we implemented two important features for our application. The first feature was enabling users to vote for their favorite bookmarks and browse popular bookmarks. The second feature was allowing users to comment on bookmarks. These two features mean that users can discover new interesting bookmarks and communicate with each other, which has emphasized the social aspect of our application. During the course of this chapter, we learned about several new Django features, including the Django comments application.

The next chapter switches to a new topic. Sooner or later, you will need an administration interface for your application to manage your data models. Fortunately, Django comes with a fully fledged administration interface ready to be used. We will learn how to enable and customize this interface in the next section, so continue to read!

8
Creating an Administration Interface

Sooner or later, we will need an administration interface to manage the content that users post to our web site. In fact, the administration interface is a universal feature needed in any web application that stores and manages data. For this reason, Django comes with a fully fledged administration interface ready to be used. This administration interface is considered one of the coolest features in Django because it's easy to use, and yet is powerful and flexible.

In this chapter you will learn how to:

- Activate the administration interface
- Use the administration interface to manage content
- Customize the administration interface
- Assign permissions to users and groups

Activating the administration interface

The administration interface comes as a Django application. To activate it, we will follow a simple procedure that is similar to enabling the user authentication system.

The administration application is located in the `django.contrib.admin` package. So the first step is adding the path of this package to the `INSTALLED_APPS` variable. Open the `settings.py` file, locate `INSTALLED_APPS`, and edit it as follows:

```
INSTALLED_APPS = (
    'django.contrib.auth',
    'django.contrib.admin',
    'django.contrib.contenttypes',
```

```
        'django.contrib.sessions',
        'django.contrib.sites',
        'django.contrib.comments',
        'django_bookmarks.bookmarks',
)
```

Next, run the following command to create the necessary tables for the administration application:

$ python manage.py syncdb

Now we need to make the administration interface accessible from within our site by adding URL entries for it. The admin application defines many views (as we will see later), so manually adding a separate entry for each view can become a tedious task. Therefore, the admin interface provides a shortcut for this. There is a single object that encapsulates all the admin views. To use it, open the urls.py file and edit it as follows:

```
from django.contrib import admin
admin.autodiscover()
urlpatterns = ('',
  [...]
  # Admin interface
  (r'^admin/(.*)', admin.site.root),
)
```

Here, we are importing the admin module, calling a method in it, and mapping all the URLs under the path ^admin/ to a view called admin.site.root. This will make the views of the administration interface accessible from within our project.

One last thing remains before we see the administration page in action. We need to tell Django what models can be managed in the administration interface. This is done by creating a new file called the admin.py file in the bookmarks directory. Create the bookmarks/admin.py file and add the following code to it:

```
from django.contrib import admin
from bookmarks.models import *
class LinkAdmin(admin.ModelAdmin):
  pass
admin.site.register(Link, LinkAdmin)
```

We created a class derived from the admin.ModelAdmin class and mapped it to the Link model using the admin.site.register method. This effectively tells Django to enable the Link model in the administration interface. The keyword pass means that the class is empty. Later, we will use this class to customize the administration page; so it won't remain empty.

Do the same to the `Bookmark` , `Tag`, and `SharedBookmark` models and add it to the
`bookmarks/admin.py` file. Now, create an empty admin class for each of them and
register it. The `User` model is provided by Django and, therefore, we don't have
control over it. But fortunately, it already has an `Admin` class so it's available in
the administration interface by default.

Next, launch the development server and direct your browser to
`http://127.0.0.1:8000/admin/`. You will be greeted by a login page.
Remember when we created a superuser account after writing the database model
earlier in this book? This is the account that you have to use in order to log in:

Django administration

Username:

Password:

Log in

Next, you will see a list of the models that are available to the administration
interface. As discussed earlier, only models that have admin classes in the
`bookmarks/admin.py` file will appear on this page.

Django administration — Welcome, ayman. Change password / Log out

Site administration

Auth
Groups   Add Change   Recent Actions
Users   Add Change   My Actions
                          None available
Bookmarks
Bookmarks Add Change
Links   Add Change
Tags   Add Change
Comments
Comments Add Change
Sites
Sites   Add Change

If you click on a model name, you will get a list of the objects that are stored in the database under this model. You can use this page to view or edit a particular object, or to add a new one. The following figure shows the listing page for the Link model:

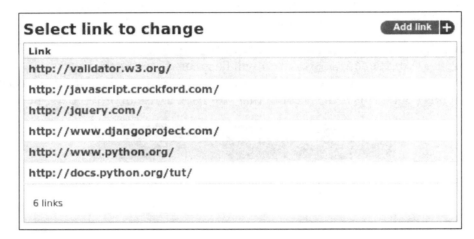

The edit form is generated according to the fields that exist in the model. The Link form, for example, contains a single text field called Url. You can use this form to view and change the URL of a Link object. In addition, the form performs proper validation of fields before saving the object. So if you try to save a Link object with an invalid URL, you will receive an error message asking you to correct the field. The following figure shows a validation error when trying to save an invalid link:

Fields are mapped to form widgets according to their type. For example, date fields are edited using a calendar widget, whereas foreign key fields are edited using a list widget, and so on. The following figure shows a calendar widget from the user edit page. Django uses it for date and time fields.

As you may have noticed, the administration interface represents models by using the string returned by the __unicode__ method. It was indeed a good idea to replace the generic strings returned by the default __unicode__ method with more helpful ones. This greatly helps when working with the administration page, as well as with debugging.

Experiment with the administration pages. Try to create, edit, and delete objects. Notice how changes made in the administration interface are immediately reflected on the live site. Also, the administration interface keeps a track of the actions that you make and lets you review the history of changes for each object.

This section has covered most of what you need to know in order to use the administration interface provided by Django. This feature is actually one of the main advantages of using Django. You get a fully featured administration interface from writing only a few lines of code!

Next, we will see how to tweak and customize the administration pages. As a bonus, we will learn more about the permissions system offered by Django.

Customizing the administration interface

The administration interface provided by Django is very powerful and flexible. Activating it only takes a couple of minutes, and this will give you a fully featured administration kit for your site. Although the administration application should be sufficient for most needs, Django offers several ways to customize and enhance it. In addition to specifying which models are available in the administration interface, you can also specify how listing pages are presented. You can even override the templates used to render the administration pages. So let's learn about these features.

Customizing listing pages

As we saw in the previous section, we defined admin classes in a file called admin.py to mark data models as available in the administration interface. These classes are also useful in customizing several aspects of the administration pages.

Let's learn about this with examples. The listing page of bookmarks displays the string representation of each bookmark, as we can see in the following figure:

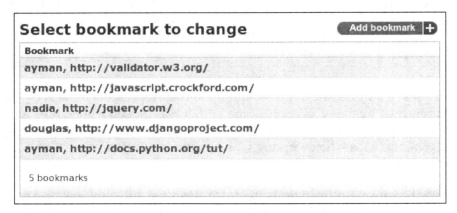

Wouldn't this page be more useful if it displayed the URL, title, and the owner of the bookmark in separate columns? It turns out that implementing this only requires a single line of code. Edit the BookmarkAdmin class in the bookmarks/admin.py file and replace pass in the body of the BookmarkAdmin class with the following highlighted line of code:

```
class BookmarkAdmin(admin.ModelAdmin):
    list_display = ('title', 'link', 'user')
```

Now refresh the same page and notice the changes.

Title	Link	User
W3C Validation Service	http://validator.w3.org/	ayman
JavaScript Tips	http://javascript.crockford.com/	ayman
jQuery	http://jquery.com/	nadia
Django Web Framework	http://www.djangoproject.com/	douglas
Python Tutorial	http://docs.python.org/tut/	ayman

5 bookmarks

The table is organized much better now. We simply defined a tuple attribute called `list_display` in the `BookmarkAdmin` class. This tuple contains the names of fields to be used in the listing page.

Following are other attributes that we can define in admin classes; each one should be defined as a tuple of one or more field names:

- `list_filter`: If this attribute is defined, it creates a sidebar with links that can be used to filter objects according to one or more fields in the model.
- `ordering`: These fields are used to order objects in the listing page. If the field name is preceded by a minus sign, descending order is used instead of ascending order.
- `search_fields`: If this attribute is defined, it creates a search field that can be used to search available objects in the data model according to one or more fields.

Let's utilize each of these attributes in the bookmark listing page. Again, edit the `BookmarkAdmin` model in the `bookmarks/admin.py` file and append the following highlighted lines of code:

```
class BookmarkAdmin(admin.ModelAdmin):
    list_display = ('title', 'link', 'user')
    list_filter = ('user',)
    ordering = ('title',)
    search_fields = ('title',)
```

These new attributes provide the following features:

- `list_filter` : Enables us to filter bookmarks by user
- `ordering` : Orders bookmarks by title
- `search_fields` : Allows us to search bookmarks by title

Now, refresh the bookmark listing page again to see the changes:

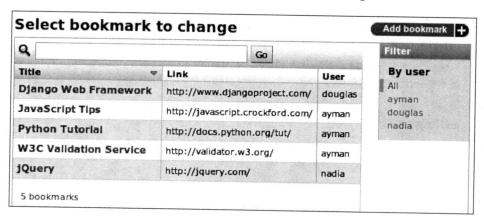

As you can see, we were able to customize and enhance the bookmark listing page with only a few lines of code. Next, we will learn about customizing the templates used to render administration pages, which will give us an even greater control over the administration interface.

Overriding administration templates

There are times when you want to change the look and feel of the administration interface, or to move the elements on the various administration pages and rearrange them. Fortunately, the administration interface is flexible enough to do all this and more by allowing us to override its templates.

The process of customizing an administration template is simple. First, you copy the template from the administration application folder to your project's templates folder, and then you edit this template and customize it to your liking. The location of the administration templates depends on where Django is installed. Here is a list of the default installation paths of Django under the major operating systems (`X.X` is the version of Python on your system):

- Windows: `C:\PythonXX\Lib\site-packages\django`
- UNIX and Linux: `/usr/lib/pythonX.X/site-packages/django`
- Mac OS X: `/Library/Python/X.X/site-packages/django`

If you cannot find Django in the default installation path for your operating system, perform a file system search for `django-admin.py`. You will get multiple hits, but the one that you want will be under the Django installation path, inside a folder called `bin`.

After locating the Django installation path, open `django/contrib/admin/templates/`, and you will find the templates used by the administration application. There are many files in this directory, but the most important ones are:

- `admin/base_site.html`: This is the base template for the administration interface. All the pages inherit from this template.
- `admin/change_list.html`: This template generates a list of available objects in a particular model.
- `admin/change_form.html`: This template generates a form for adding or editing an object.
- `admin/delete_confirmation.html`: This template generates the confirmation page when deleting an object.

Let's try to customize one of these templates. Suppose that we want to change the string **Django administration** located at the top of all admin pages. To do so, create a folder called `admin` inside the `templates` folder of our project, and copy the `admin/base_site.html` file to it. After that, edit the file to change all instances of `Django` to `Django Bookmarks`:

```
{% extends "admin/base.html" %}
{% load i18n %}
{% block title %}{{ title }} |
    {% trans 'Django Bookmarks site admin' %}{% endblock %}
{% block branding %}
<h1 id="site-name">
    {% trans 'Django Bookmarks administration' %}</h1>
{% endblock %}
{% block nav-global %}{% endblock %}
```

Refresh the administration interface in your browser to see the changes:

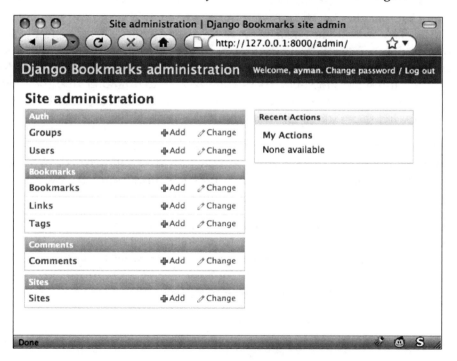

The process was pretty simple, wasn't it? Feel free to experiment with other templates. For example, you may want to add a help message to listing or edit pages. The administration templates make use of many advanced features of the Django template system. So, if you see a template tag that you are not familiar with, you can refer to the Django documentation.

Users, groups, and permissions

So far, we have been logged into the administration interface using the superuser account that we created with `manage.py syncdb`. In reality, however, you may have other trusted users who need access to the administration page. In this section, we will see how to allow other users to use the administration interface. We will also learn more about the Django permissions system in the process.

Before we continue, I want to emphasize that only trusted users should be given access to the administration pages. The administration interface is a very powerful tool, so only those whom you know well should be granted access to it.

User permissions

If you don't have users in the database other than the superuser, create a new user account using the registration form that we built in Chapter 4. Alternatively, you could use the administration interface by clicking on **Users | Add User**. Next, return to the **Users** list and click on the name of the newly created user. You will get a form which can be used to edit various aspects of the user account such as name and email information. Under the **Permissions** section of the edit form, you will find a checkbox labelled **Staff status**. Enabling this checkbox will let the new user enter the administration interface. However, they won't be able to do much after they log in because this checkbox only grants access to the administration area, and it does not give the ability to see or change the data models.

To give permission to the new user to change the data models, you can enable the **superuser status** checkbox, which will grant the new user full permission to perform any function that he or she wants. This option makes the account as powerful as the superuser account created by `manage.py syncdb`.

However, on the whole, it's not desirable to grant a user full access to everything. Therefore, Django gives you the ability to have fine control over what users can do through the permissions system. Below the **Superuser status** checkbox, you will find a list of permissions that you can grant to the user. If you examine this list, you will find that each data model has three types of permissions:

- Adding an object to the data model
- Changing an object in the data model
- Deleting an object from the data model

These permissions are automatically generated by Django for data models that contain an Admin class. Use the arrow button to grant some permission to the account that we are editing. For example, give the account the ability to add, edit, and delete—links, tags, and bookmarks. Next, log out and then log into the administration interface again using the new account. You will notice that you will only be able to manage the Link, Tag, and Bookmark data models.

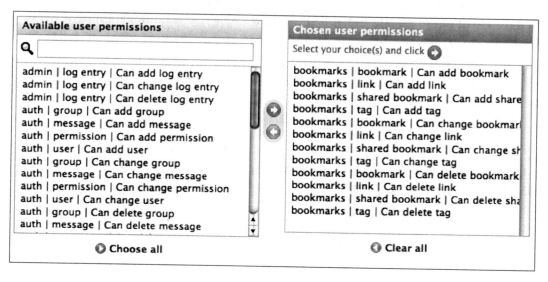

The permissions section of the user edit page also contains a checkbox called **Active**. This checkbox can be used as a global switch to enable and disable the account. When unchecked, the user won't be able to log into the main site or the administration area.

Group permissions

If you have a considerable number of users who share the same permissions, it would be a tedious and error-prone task to edit each user's account and assign the same permissions to them. Therefore, Django provides another user management facility—groups. To put it simply, groups are a way of categorizing users who share the same permissions. You can create a group and assign permissions to it. And when you add a user to the group, this user is granted all of the group's permissions.

Creating a group is not any different from other data models. Click **Groups** on the main page of the administration interface, and then click on **Add Group**. Next, enter a group name and assign some permissions to the group. Finally, click **Save**.

To add a user to a group, edit the user account, scroll to the **Groups** section in the edit form, and select whichever group you want to add the user to.

Using permissions in views

Though we have only used permissions in the administration interface so far, Django also lets us utilize the permission system while writing views. When programming a view, it is possible to use permissions to grant a group of users access to a particular feature or a page, such as private content. We will learn about methods that can be used to do so in this section. We won't actually make changes to the code of our application, but feel free to do so if you want to experiment with the methods explained.

If you wanted to check whether a user has a particular permission, you could use the `has_perm` method on the `User` object. This method takes a string that represents the permission in the following format:

```
app.operation_model
```

`app` is the name of the application where the model is located; `operation` is either add, change, or delete; and `model` is the name of the model. For example, to check whether the user can add tags, use:

```
user.has_perm('bookmarks.add_tag')
```

And to check if the user can change bookmarks:

```
user.has_perm('bookmarks.change_bookmark')
```

Furthermore, Django provides a decorator that can be used to restrict a view to the users who have a particular permission. The decorator is called `permission_required` and is located in the `django.contrib.auth.decorators` package.

Using this decorator is similar to how we used the `login_required` decorator to restrict pages to the logged-in users. Let's say we want to restrict the `bookmark_save_page` view (in the `bookmarks/views.py` file) to users who have the `bookmarks.add_bookmark` permission. To do so, we can use the following code:

```
from django.contrib.auth.decorators import permission_required
@permission_required('bookmarks.add_bookmark')
def bookmark_save_page(request):
    [...]
```

This decorator takes two parameters: the permission to check for, and where to redirect users if they don't have the required permission.

The question of whether to use the `has_perm` method or the `permission_required` decorator depends on the level of control that you want. If you need to control access to a view as a whole, use the `permission_required` decorator. However, if you need finer control over permissions inside a view, use the `has_perm` method. These two approaches should be sufficient for any permission-related needs.

Summary

Though this chapter is relatively short, we learned how to implement a lot of things. This emphasizes the fact that Django lets you do a lot with only a few lines of code. You learned how to utilize Django's powerful administration interface, customize it, and take advantage of the comprehensive permission system.

Here is a quick summary of the features covered in this chapter.

- Activating the administration interface consists of the following steps:
  - Add the `django.contrib.admin` application to `INSTALLED_APPS` in the `settings.py` file
  - Run the `manage.py syncdb` command to create the administration application tables
  - Add URL entries for the administration pages to the `urls.py` file
  - For each model that you want to manage through the administration interface, add a corresponding admin class and register it in the `admin.py` file

- You can customize listing pages in the administration interface by adding one or more of the following fields to the admin class: `list_display`, `list_filter`, `ordering`, and `search_fields`

- You can check whether a user has a particular permission by using the `has_perm` method on the `User` object

- You can restrict a view to users who have a particular permission by using the `permission_required` decorator from the `django.contrib.auth.decorators` package

In the next chapter, you will learn about several exciting features found in almost every Web 2.0 application these days; namely, RSS feeds, browsing popular content, and searching. So, keep reading!

9
Advanced Browsing and Searching

Providing users with many ways to browse content is always a good idea, as it makes your application appeal to a broader audience. Different users will have different ways of getting content. Some users prefer to browse available content for interesting items, whereas others would rather search for particular topics. Some users may even prefer to receive new content when it becomes available instead of searching for it.

Given how feed readers have become popular tools among web users to monitor updates, we will begin this chapter by learning about web feed technology and how to utilize the Django feed framework to construct feeds for our application. This will enable users to subscribe to our feeds and receive content updates whenever they are available. Next, we will improve our search feature to provide more accurate results, learning more about the Django database API in the process. Finally, we will enhance the usability of bookmark-listing views by splitting long lists into multiple pages. As you will see, this chapter covers many interesting topics and carries numerous improvements to our application, so please read on!

In this chapter, you will learn about the following:

- Adding RSS feeds
- Advanced searching
- Organizing content into pages (pagination)

Adding RSS feeds

With the widespread use of frequently updated web sites such as blogs, wikis, and social bookmarking sites, users had to keep up with updates on many web sites using their web browsers on a daily basis. But as the task of keeping up with numerous web sites became tedious, the need arose for more efficient methods to track updates. Fortunately, a technology called web feeds already existed for providing users with frequently updated content. The concept behind this technology is simple:

- An XML document containing the latest updates is published on the web site. This document is called a **web feed**

- Users can take advantage of this document by subscribing to it, using a specialized program called a **feed reader** or **aggregator**

- This program polls the feed on a regular basis and notifies the user when updates are available

Web feeds became an efficient and easy solution for tracking updates, and the technology of feeds and aggregators quickly spread among web sites and users. These days, offering feeds is a standard feature in Web 2.0 applications. There are feeds for the latest content, feeds for popular content, feeds for content under a specific category, and so on. In addition, aggregator programs have been incorporated into major web browsers and email clients.

With the above in mind, it's natural for us to think of adding feed support to our application, as there are many ways to benefit from this technology in our project. For example, we can offer feeds for the latest bookmarks, bookmarks posted by a particular user, or bookmarks that are posted under a specific tag. The possibilities are numerous, and creating a feed in Django is easy. It works in the same way regardless of the number and types of feeds that we want to add. Django provides a very powerful framework for creating web feeds. To create a feed, you simply define a Python class and leave the rest to Django. In this section, you will learn about this framework by creating two types of feeds: one for the latest bookmarks posted to the site, and one for the bookmarks posted by a specific user. After you finish reading this section, you will be able to utilize the Django feed framework to create any feed that you can think of, so let's get started!

Creating the recent bookmarks feed

Our first feed will list the latest 10 bookmarks posted to the site. You should already know by now that you can retrieve the latest 10 bookmarks from the database using the following method call (as we saw in Chapter 6):

```
Bookmark.objects.order_by('-id')[:10]
```

This method sorts bookmarks by `id` in descending order, and obtains the first 10 results. As we can see, turning this method call into a web feed only takes a few lines of code.

The first step in defining a feed is creating a class that is derived from the `Feed` class. This class is a part of the feed framework located at `django.contrib.syndication`. To keep our source code organized, we will add a new file for feed classes. Create a file called `feeds.py` in the `bookmarks` directory, and insert the following class into it:

```
from django.contrib.syndication.feeds import Feed
from bookmarks.models import Bookmark

class RecentBookmarks(Feed):
  title = u'Django Bookmarks | Recent Bookmarks'
  link = '/feeds/recent/'
  description = u'Recent bookmarks posted to Django Bookmarks'

  def items(self):
    return Bookmark.objects.order_by('-id')[:10]
```

Let's go through this code line by line:

- We first import the `Feed` class, which should be the base class for all feeds.
- We also import the `Bookmark` model because we will need it for generating the most recent bookmarks list.
- Next, we define a class called `RecentBookmarks` derived from `Feed`.
- We define three attributes in this class: the title of the feed, the link (URL) of the feed, and a short description of the purpose of the feed.
- Finally, we define a method named `items` that returns the items of the feed. Since we want this field to list the most recent 10 bookmarks, we use the method call that we wrote earlier in this section to retrieve this list of bookmarks.

There are several feed formats available, but the most common one is RSS; and Django uses this by default. An RSS feed consists of two sections:

- A section that describes the feed by providing its title, link, description, and several other possible properties. These properties can be set by defining attributes in the feed class.
- A section that lists the items of the feed. Each item consists of a title, link, description, and several other possible fields. We will see how to define these next.

The `items` method in our feed class returns a list of `Bookmark` objects. So how will Django map a `Bookmark` object to the item fields just mentioned? For the title and description, Django uses the object's string representation. For the link, it calls a method named `get_absolute_url` on the object to get the link of the item. Needless to say, Django is flexible enough to let us customize these default assumptions.

Let's start with the link to the item. Open the `bookmarks/models.py` file and add the highlighted method to the `Bookmark` data model:

```
class Bookmark(models.Model):
   title = models.CharField(max_length=200)
   user = models.ForeignKey(User)
   link = models.ForeignKey(Link)
   def __unicode__(self):
      return u'%s, %s' % (self.user.username, self.link.url)
   def get_absolute_url(self):
      return self.link.url
```

This method is simple; it returns the URL of the bookmark. We will let Django use the string representation of the bookmark as the title for now, and get back to customizing this later.

The last step in adding a feed is creating a URL entry for it. Because we are using the Django feed framework to generate our feeds, we add this URL entry in a special way. We map a URL to a view provided by the `django.contrib.syndication` package, and pass our feeds to this view using a dictionary. This is better explained with action, so open the `urls.py` file and add the highlighted lines to it:

```
import os.path
from django.conf.urls.defaults import *
from django.views.generic.simple import direct_to_template
from django.contrib import admin
from bookmarks.views import *
from bookmarks.feeds import *

admin.autodiscover()

site_media = os.path.join(
   os.path.dirname(__file__), 'site_media'
)

# Make sure you add the feeds dict before
# the urlpatterns object.
feeds = {
   'recent': RecentBookmarks
}

urlpatterns = patterns('',
```

```
[...]
# Feeds
(r'^feeds/(?P<url>.*)/$',
 'django.contrib.syndication.views.feed',
 {'feed_dict': feeds}),
)
```

We imported the newly created `feeds` module and defined a dictionary called `feeds`. This dictionary maps each feed class to its URL. After that, we added a new URL entry, which maps all URLs that start with `feeds/` to the `feed` view (from `django.contrib.syndication.views`). The third element of the URL entry passes extra arguments to the view, and in this case, it passes the `feeds` dictionary that we defined earlier.

This may seem a bit complicated, but actually it's simple once we see how it works:

- We map all URLs under `^feeds/` to a view provided by the feed framework. We also pass a dictionary that contains our feeds to this view.
- When a URL such as `^feeds/recent/$` is requested, the `feed` view is invoked. This view looks up the part of the URL after `^feeds/` in the `feeds` dictionary to retrieve the corresponding feed class.
- Next, the view generates the XML code of the feed and returns it to the user.

Let's try our new feed. Launch the development server and point your browser to `http://127.0.0.1:8000/feeds/recent/`. The result depends on your browser. If you are using Firefox, you should see something similar to the following:

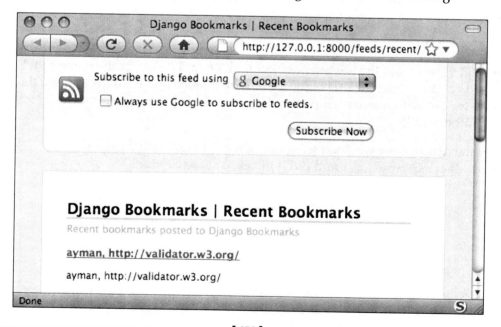

It worked! Django used the string representation of bookmarks for item title and description, but it's working nonetheless and the links are correct. As you may have thought already, the string representation of bookmarks is helpful while debugging, but not very user-friendly. So we will customize this next.

Customizing item fields

Item fields can be customized using templates. You can customize them by changing the title of an item, adding a description to it, specifying an author, and so on. The framework looks for feed templates in a directory called `feeds`. When you create templates in this directory, they will be automatically picked up by the feed framework. Such templates should use the following naming format:

```
feedname_fieldname.html
```

Let's learn how to do this with an example. To customize the titles of feed items in the recent bookmarks feed, you should use a template called `recent_title.html`. If you compare this name with the naming format above, you can see that `feedname` in the format is the name of the feed as it appears in the `feeds` dictionary, which we added to the `urls.py` file. In the case of the `RecentBookmarks` feed, the name is `recent`. You can also see that `fieldname` is the name of the item field that you want to customize. Since we want to customize the titles of feed items, `fieldname` here is `title`.

To see this in action, create a directory named `feeds` in the `templates` directory, create a template called `recent_title.html` in this directory, and insert the following code into the template:

```
{{ obj.title }}
```

The `feed` view passes the `Bookmark` object to the template under the name `obj`. So we used `obj` to output the title of the bookmark. Notice that we didn't escape the title here as we did with regular templates; the reason is that the feed framework escapes input automatically.

As for the description, we don't want any. Create an empty file named `recent_description.html` and put it in `templates/feeds/`.

After creating both files, refresh the feed in your browser to see the changes:

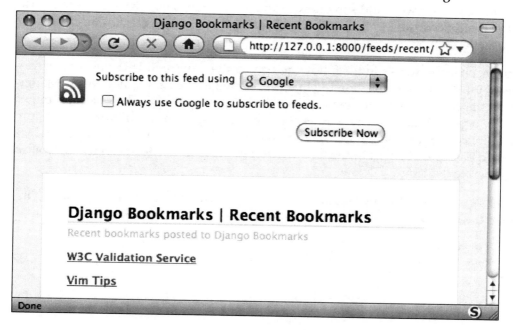

That's much better! The user now has an idea about the contents of the link. Feel free to customize the feed further by offering more information. For example, you can put the owner of the bookmark and its tags in the description template.

With this, we finish implementing our first feed. Next, we will implement a feed that lists bookmarks for a specific user. This is going to be a more advanced feed, because it takes the username as a parameter in the URL.

Creating the user bookmarks feed

In addition to tracking new bookmarks posted to the site, our users may want to track bookmarks posted by specific users. For instance, one user may want to keep an eye on the bookmarks posted by their friends. Therefore, it would be a good idea to provide a feed for each user; this feed lists the bookmarks posted by this user only.

Implementing this type of feed is slightly more involved than the previous one. That's because the username will be passed as a part of the feed URL, and the items of the feed will change according to the requested username.

It is neither reasonable, nor feasible to write a separate feed class for each user. It would be great if we could somehow examine the requested URL and generate the list of items according to it. Guess what? Django provides an elegant mechanism to do exactly that!

This mechanism works in the following way: If the requested URL contains extra bits of information in addition to what is specified in the feeds dictionary, Django understands that the requested feed is associated with a particular object (in our case, a User object). Django retrieves this object by passing the extra bits of information (in our case, the username) to a method named get_object in the feed object. Next, Django passes this object to the feed when rendering it. The feed can use this object to generate its items.

So let's go through this by creating a class for the user feed and then examining it. Open the bookmarks/feeds.py file and append the following class to it:

```python
from django.core.exceptions import ObjectDoesNotExist
from django.contrib.auth.models import User

class UserBookmarks(Feed):
  def get_object(self, bits):
    if len(bits) != 1:
      raise ObjectDoesNotExist
    return User.objects.get(username=bits[0])

  def title(self, user):
    return (
      u'Django Bookmarks | Bookmarks for %s' % user.username
    )

  def link(self, user):
    return '/feeds/user/%s/' % user.username

  def description(self, user):
    return u'Recent bookmarks posted by %s' % user.username

  def items(self, user):
    return user.bookmark_set.order_by('-id')[:10]
```

We will go through each method in this class:

- get_object: Django calls this method if the requested URL contains extra bits of information. This information is passed in the bits parameter, which is an array of strings that result from splitting the additional part of the URL by the character /. For example, if we map this feed class to the URL ^feeds/user/$ and the URL ^feeds/user/param1/param2/$ is requested, the bits parameter will be ['param1', 'param2'].

- `get_object`: This method returns the object that is associated with the feed. This feed expects only one element in the `bits` variable (the username) and returns the `User` object for this username. If the `bits` variable does not contain one element, or if a `User` object does not exist for the specified username, we raise an exception which causes Django to generate a 404 page not found error.

- `title`, `link`, `description`: In the first feed, these were simple class attributes. Now they are methods. We did so because we also want the title, link, and description of the feed to change depending on the requested username. Django is smart enough to understand whether we defined these feed properties as attributes or methods. If we use a method, it passes the associated object of the feed to the method.

- `items`: This method also receives the `User` object associated with the feed, and uses it to generate the list of bookmarks.

After writing the feed class, we should add it to the `feeds` dictionary. So open the `urls.py` file and add the highlighted line to it:

```
import os.path
from django.conf.urls.defaults import *
from django.views.generic.simple import direct_to_template
from django.contrib import admin
from bookmarks.views import *
from bookmarks.feeds import *

admin.autodiscover()

site_media = os.path.join(
  os.path.dirname(__file__),
  'site_media'
)

feeds = {
  'recent': RecentBookmarks,
  'user': UserBookmarks
}
```

Next, we will create templates for this `user` feed and it is similar to what we did previously. Add a file called `user_title.html` with the following contents to `templates/feeds/`:

```
{{ obj.title }}
```

Finally, we will create an empty file called `user_description.html` in the same directory.

Now that our feed is ready, navigate to `http://127.0.0.1:8000/feeds/user/` `your_username/` (replacing `your_username` with your actual username) to see the feed:

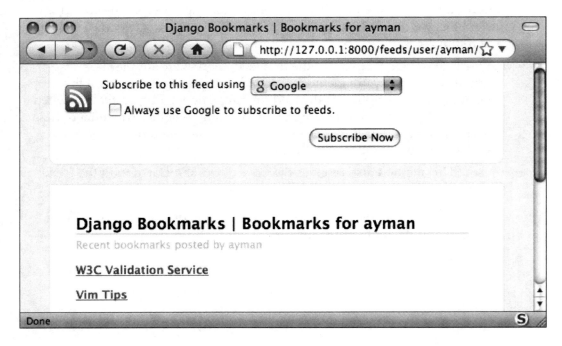

Linking feeds to HTML pages

We now have functional web feeds that are ready to be used. But how do we make our users aware of the existence of these feeds? One way is to simply create an HTML link to the feed URL, preferably using the standard feed icons that are commonly used on the Web (you can obtain them from `http://www.feedicons.` `com/`). However, automated bots and feed readers may not be able to discover your feed if you merely place a regular link to it in your page. Therefore, there is a special HTML markup that you can put in the head section of the HTML page to tell programs that this page has a corresponding web feed. Let's learn about this markup by using it to link our main page to the recent bookmarks feed. Open the `templates/main_page.html` file and change it by adding the highlighted lines as follows:

```
{% extends "base.html" %}
{% block title %}Welcome to Django Bookmarks{% endblock %}
{% block head %}Welcome to Django Bookmarks{% endblock %}
{% block external %}
  <link rel="alternate" type="application/rss+xml"
```

```
        title="Django Bookmarks | Recent Bookmarks"
        href="/feeds/recent/" />
{% endblock %}
[...]
```

The `link` tag in the head section tells feed-aware programs that your HTML page has an associated feed. If you navigate your browser to the main page of your application using the Firefox web browser, you will notice that Firefox displays a feed icon to the right of the URL of the site. If you click this icon, you will be taken to the feed page where you can subscribe to it:

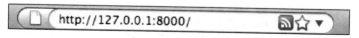

Let's add a similar link tag to the user page. Open the `templates/user_page.html` file and insert the highlighted line into it as follows:

```
{% extends "base.html" %}
{% block external %}
  <script type="text/javascript"
    src="/site_media/bookmark_edit.js"><script>
  <link rel="alternate" type="application/rss+xml"
    title="Django Bookmarks | Bookmarks for {{ username }}"
    href="/feeds/user/{{ username }}" />
{% endblock %}
```

That was fun, wasn't it? I find it particularly interesting that we added a completely new feature to our project by writing minimal lines of code and without any major changes to our existing code. Django boosts the developer productivity to its maximum by offering powerful and easy-to-use tools such as the feed framework. Feel free to continue exploring this framework. For example, you can try to create a feed that lists recent tags or recent bookmarks under a specific tag.

In the next section, we will enhance the search feature that was added in Chapter 6. This feature is particularly important because it is needed in almost any web application, and also because users often think of using it to locate content that they saw before or to discover new content that interests them.

Advanced searching

In Chapter 6, we built a simple search feature into our project. We did so to learn more about AJAX and live form processing. The search page returns bookmarks that contain the query string in the title and it is implemented using the `filter` method of the model API. This line of code does the actual searching in our search view:

```
bookmarks = Bookmark.objects.filter(title__icontains=query)
```

This was sufficient to get a basic search page working. However, things are not this simple in reality. To see why, let's say that a user entered "AJAX advantages" into the search box. If the database contains a bookmark with the string "AJAX advantages" in its title, it will be returned in the search results. However, if there is a bookmark titled "Advantages of AJAX", it won't be returned, though it's obviously relevant to the search query.

As illustrated by this example, searching for titles that contain the exact query string does not produce satisfactory results. We should split the query string into key words and search for titles that contain all of these key words.

In this section, we will improve upon the search feature in our application and overcome the problem just described. But before we can do so, we need to learn more about the Django database API.

Retrieving objects with the database API

So far, in our application we have used several techniques to retrieve objects from data models. All of these techniques work by calling methods on the `objects` attribute of a data model. This attribute is called the **manager** of the data model, and it is the interface through which database queries are made.

Some of the methods that we used on the manager include:

- `get`: It retrieves an object by a unique field
- `all`: It retrieves all of the objects in the model
- `count`: It returns the number of objects
- `filter`: It can be used to construct queries that are similar to SQL `SELECT` statements
- `order_by`: It lets you provide the sorting order of returned objects

In this section, we will learn more about the Django database API. But before we proceed, it is a good idea to add some bookmarks with the following properties so that you can get the most out of the following examples:

- A bookmark with a URL that begins with `https`
- A bookmark with a URL that begins with `https` and ends with `html`
- A bookmark with the tag `JavaScript`
- A bookmark with the tags `JavaScript` and `Web`
- A bookmark with the word `JavaScript` in its title
- A bookmark with the word `JavaScript` in its title and the tag `Web`

The `filter` method is very powerful. It provides a variety of ways to query your data model. Queries are constructed by passing keyword arguments to the method. For example, if you want to search for all links that start with `https`, you can use the following command. (Note that this and all the following commands include **two** underscores):

```
>>> Link.objects.filter(url__istartswith='https')
```

You can launch the interactive console to test these method calls by running the following command:
```
$ python manage.py shell
```
Don't forget to import the project's models from
`bookmarks.models import *`.

You can pass multiple keyword arguments to the `filter` method and it will join them together using the logical operator "and", meaning that only objects that satisfy all arguments are returned. For example, the following method call will return all links that start with `https` and end with `html`:

```
>>> Link.objects.filter(
    url__istartswith='https', url__iendswith='html')
```

You can also use the `filter` method to do queries that span multiple data models. Let's say we want to retrieve all `Bookmark` objects whose link starts with `https`. The following method call does not work and raises an exception:

```
>>> Bookmark.objects.filter(link__istartswith='https')
```

This happens because the `link` field in the `Bookmark` data model is a `Link` object, and not a regular string. To construct this query we need to access the `url` field of the `link` field. This can be done like this:

```
>>> Bookmark.objects.filter(link__url__istartswith='https')
```

To access the `url` attribute of the link field, we used **two** underscore characters. You can do so as many times as you want to go deeper into the object structure.

While working with queries that span multiple data models, you may come across a problem that is illustrated by the following example: the `Bookmark` and `Tag` models are related. The relationship field resides in the `Tag` model. How do we construct a query that retrieves bookmarks according to their associated `Tag` objects? Let's say we want to get all bookmarks with the `JavaScript` tag. This can be done as follows:

```
>>> Bookmark.objects.filter(
    tag__name__iexact='JavaScript')
```

We used the model name as the first part of the keyword argument. This allows us to perform relationship queries even if the relationship field resides in the other model.

`all`, `filter`, and `order_by` return an object that looks and acts like a list. However, its type is actually a special Django class called `QuerySet`. This class represents a collection of objects and contains methods that can be used to further refine your search criteria.

The following constructs a query set that contains all bookmarks with "JavaScript" in the title, and then refines the search only to include bookmarks owned by the user `ayman`:

```
>>> query_set = Bookmark.objects.filter(
    tag__name__iexact='JavaScript')
>>> bookmarks = query_set.filter(
    user__username__iexact='ayman')
```

This can also be done in one line using method chaining:

```
>>> bookmarks = Bookmark.objects.filter(
    tag__name__iexact='JavaScript').filter(
    user__username__iexact='ayman')
```

The real power of method chaining becomes clear when we combine `filter` with another method called `exclude`. This method, as the name suggests, removes objects that match the passed keyword arguments. Let's say you want all bookmarks that contain "Python" in the title, except for those which are tagged with "Web." You can do so by using the following method chain:

```
>>> Bookmark.objects.filter(
    title__icontains='JavaScript').exclude(
    tag__name__iexact='Web')
```

Method chaining is also useful if you want to retrieve a list of objects with `filter` and then sort the list. The following method chain obtains all bookmarks that are owned by user `ayman` and sorts them according to the title:

```
>>> Bookmark.objects.filter(user__username__iexact='ayman')
                    .order_by('title')
```

When you are querying a data model that is expected to contain a large number of elements, it is recommended to only retrieve a limited number of objects instead of getting the whole result set. If you do so, you avoid overloading the database system. Specifying how many items you want is done using the standard Python index syntax. For example, to retrieve the first 10 bookmarks, you can do the following:

```
>>> Bookmark.objects.all()[:10]
```

This is possible because a `QuerySet` object doesn't actually retrieve objects from the database when you create it. They only do so when you try to access its items.

Advanced queries with Q objects

We can filter objects according to multiple conditions by passing more than one keyword argument to the `filter` method or using method chaining. In either case, the conditions are joined together using the "and" logical operator. But what if we want to use the "or" logical operator, or construct complex queries that use both operators? Django provides a special class called Q that let us do this.

To put it simply, a Q object encapsulates one or more keyword arguments. You can use it to construct complex conditions, and then pass it to `filter` or `exclude`. The constructor of Q objects takes keyword arguments exactly like `filter` and `exclude`. The power of Q objects come from the fact that they support | and & operators. Let's see this in action by using an example. The following call returns bookmarks with `Python` or `JavaScript` in their titles:

```
>>> from django.db.models import Q
>>> q1 = Q(title__icontains='Python')
>>> q2 = Q(title__icontains='JavaScript')
>>> q3 = q1 | q2
>>> Bookmark.objects.filter(q3)
```

We combined q1 and q2 using the | operator, which effectively creates a new Q object that matches the conditions of q1 or q2. After that, we pass the resulting Q object to `filter`. Of course, we could have done the above in one line:

```
>>> Bookmark.objects.filter(
    Q(title__icontains='Python') |
    Q(title__icontains='JavaScript'))
```

You can use the & and | operators (in addition to parentheses) to combine as many Q objects as you want. This enables you to create complex queries, which is not possible with the use of regular `filter` calls.

Now that you have a solid understanding of the Django database API, we can get back to our original task of improving the search functionality. Since querying the database is one of the most common tasks in web applications, the information in this section will be extremely valuable while working with Django. So make sure that you fully understand the methods and techniques explained here before you continue, and try to experiment with them using the interactive console. Once you are done, get ready to build a better search feature!

Improving the search feature

We've learned a lot in the previous section, so let's put our new knowledge to good use! We will improve the search feature by performing the following actions:

- Split the search query into keywords
- Construct a Q object that matches all bookmarks whose titles contain all keywords
- Retrieve the list of search results by passing the Q object to `filter`

To implement all this, open the `bookmarks/views.py` file and modify the `search_page` view, shown as follows:

```python
from django.db.models import Q

def search_page(request):
    form = SearchForm()
    bookmarks = []
    show_results = False

    if 'query' in request.GET:
        show_results = True
        query = request.GET['query'].strip()
        if query:
            keywords = query.split()
            q = Q()
            for keyword in keywords:
                q = q & Q(title__icontains=keyword)
            form = SearchForm({'query' : query})
            bookmarks = Bookmark.objects.filter(q)[:10]
    variables = RequestContext(request, {
        'form': form,
        'bookmarks': bookmarks,
        'show_results': show_results,
        'show_tags': True,
        'show_user': True
    })
    if 'ajax' in request.GET:
        return render_to_response('bookmark_list.html', variables)
    else:
        return render_to_response('search.html', variables)
```

We will examine the highlighted section line by line:

- We first split the query into key words using the `split` method.

- We construct an empty `Q` object. This object matches anything.

- We iterate through keywords creating a `Q` object for each keyword and combine it with the `Q` object from the previous iteration using the `&` ("and") operator.

- We pass the final `Q` object to `Bookmark.objects.filter` to retrieve the search results. The index syntax is used to get only the first 10 results.

Try out the new search code. If you have a bookmark titled "Python Tutorial", searching for "tutorial python" should yield this bookmark in the results.

There are many other ways to introduce additional improvements. You can, for example, add "or" based search by using the | operator. The possibilities are numerous, and you have enough information to use the Django database API and construct whatever queries you like.

The next section touches on another subject related to browsing. As time goes by, users will bookmark their favorite web pages using our application. Their bookmark lists will grow and become too large to be displayed on one page. So how can we avoid this? Pagination comes to the rescue!

Organizing content into pages (pagination)

As discussed in the previous section, it is advisable to avoid rendering large query sets into one page, as the page would increase in size and finding an item within the page would become difficult. Fortunately, there is a simple and intuitive solution to this: **pagination**. And as always, Django already has a component that implements this functionality, which is ready for us to use!

Pagination is the process of breaking content into pages. If we have a large query set of bookmarks, we split the query set into pages with 10 (or so) items on each, present the first page to the user, and provide links to browse other pages.

The Django pagination functionality is encapsulated in a class called `Paginator`, which is located in the `django.core.paginator` package. Let's learn the interface of this class using the interactive console:

```
>>> from bookmarks.models import *
>>> from django.core.paginator import Paginator
>>> query_set = Bookmark.objects.all()
>>> paginator = Paginator(query_set, 10)
```

Here we import some classes, build a query set containing all bookmarks, and instantiate a `Paginator`. The constructor of this class takes the query set to be paginated, and the number of items on each page.

Let's see how to retrieve information from the `paginator` object (of course, the results will vary depending on the amount of bookmarks that you have):

```
>>> paginator.num_pages # Number of pages
   5
>>> paginator.count  # Total number of items
   46
   # The first page (index is one-based)
>>> page = paginator.page(1)

   # Items of the first page
>>> page.object_list
[<Bookmark: ayman, http://docs.python.org/tut/>,
 <Bookmark: douglas, http://www.djangoproject.com/>,
 <Bookmark: nadia, http://jquery.com/>, ...]

   # Does the first page have a previous page?
>>> page.has_previous()
False

   # Does the first page have a next page?
>>> page.has_next()
True
```

As you can see, `Paginator` does the heavy lifting for us. It takes a query set, breaks it into pages, and enables us to render the query set into multiple pages.

Let's implement pagination into one of our views, the user page for example. Open `bookmarks/views.py` and modify the `user_page` view as highlighted here:

```
from django.core.paginator import Paginator, InvalidPage

ITEMS_PER_PAGE = 10

def user_page(request, username):
  user = get_object_or_404(User, username=username)
  query_set = user.bookmark_set.order_by('-id')
  paginator = Paginator(query_set, ITEMS_PER_PAGE)
  try:
    page_number = int(request.GET['page'])
```

```
except (KeyError, ValueError):
  page_number = 1
try:
  page = paginator.page(page_number)
except InvalidPage:
  raise Http404
bookmarks = page.object_list
variables = RequestContext(request, {
  'bookmarks': bookmarks,
  'username': username,
  'show_tags': True,
  'show_edit': username == request.user.username,
  'show_paginator': paginator.num_pages > 1,
  'has_prev': page.has_previous(),
  'has_next': page.has_next(),
  'page': page_number,
  'pages': paginator.num_pages,
  'next_page': page_number + 1,
  'prev_page': page_number - 1,
})
return render_to_response('user_page.html', variables)
```

The new changes can be broken into four sections:

We first import `Paginator` from `django.core.paginator` and define the number of items per page in a module-wide variable so that we can use it in any view. We also import an exception named `InvalidPage`, which is an exception raised by `Paginator` objects if an invalid page number is provided:

```
from django.core.paginator import Paginator, InvalidPage
ITEMS_PER_PAGE = 10
```

The `user_page` view starts by building a query set that contains all the bookmarks of the specified username and wraps the query set into a paginator:

```
query_set = user.bookmark_set.order_by('-id')
paginator = Paginator(query_set, ITEMS_PER_PAGE)
```

We try to retrieve the GET variable `page` and convert it into an integer. This may raise an exception if the variable does not exist, or if it's not an integer. In this case, we assume that the first page will be served.

After that, we get the current page using the `paginator.page`. This method raises an exception if the specified index is invalid. In this case, we generate a 404 page not found error. Then, we retrieve the bookmarks of the current page from the `page` object using the `page.object_list` attribute:

```
try:
   page_number = int(request.GET['page'])
except (KeyError, ValueError):
   page_number = 1

try:
   page = paginator.page(page)
except InvalidPage:
   raise Http404
bookmarks = page.object_list
```

We pass several new variables to the template, all of which are related to pagination:

- `show_paginator`: If the number of pages is more than one, we show a pager
- `has_prev`: If there is a page before the current page, we show a link that takes the user to the previous page
- `has_next`: The same as `has_prev`, but for the next page.
- `page`: The index of the current page
- `pages`: The total number of pages
- `next_page`: The index of the next page
- `prev_page`: The index of the previous page

```
'show_paginator': paginator.num_pages > 1,
'has_prev': page.has_previous(),
'has_next': page.has_next(),
'page': page_number,
'pages': paginator.num_pages,
'next_page': page_number + 1,
'prev_page': page_number - 1
```

Now we will update the bookmark list template in order to make use of the new pagination functionality. Open the `templates/bookmark_list.html` file and insert the highlighted section into it:

```
{% if bookmarks %}
  <ul class="bookmarks">
    {% for bookmark in bookmarks %}
      [...]
    {% endfor %}
```

```
    </ul>
    {% if show_paginator %}
      <div class="paginator">
        {% if has_prev %}
          <a href="?page={{ prev_page }}">&laquo; Previous</a>
        {% endif %}
        {% if has_next %}
          <a href="?page={{ next_page }}">Next &raquo;</a>
        {% endif %}
        (Page {{ page }} of {{ pages }})
      </div>
    {% endif %}
  {% else %}
    <p>No bookmarks found.</p>
  {% endif %}
```

The code should be easy to understand. We render the paginator if `show_paginator` is set to `True`. If there is a previous page we render a link to it, and if there is a next page, we also render a link to it. `&laquo;` and `&raquo;` are HTML entities that produce arrows that are suitable for the previous and next links respectively. Lastly, we display a short message telling the user which page they are on.

To see the paginator in action, make sure that you have enough bookmarks to trigger the rendering of a paginator (and if not, add some), and point your browser to your user page. The page should look similar to the following screenshot:

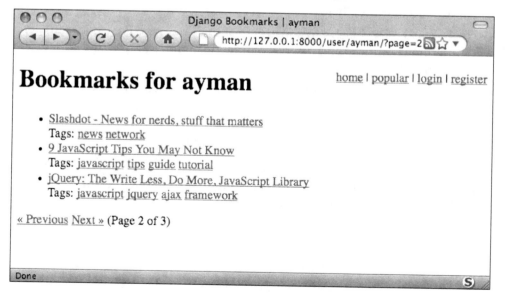

If you click on the **Next** and **Previous** buttons, you will see how bookmarks are correctly organized into pages. You will also able to improve the paginator by displaying links to individual pages between the previous and next links.

As ever, Django allowed us to improve our application and introduce a new feature quickly and easily. Pagination is very important in terms of usability and performance. Now you can add this functionality to the rest of the application views. The tag page is a good candidate, and so is the search page.

Summary

You have learned many interesting features in this chapter. You are now able to create any type of web feed with ease. You also gained a lot of information on how to use the Django database API to query data models in various ways. Finally, you learned about pagination in Django and applied it to a view in the project.

Here is a quick summary of the features covered in this chapter:

- To create a feed in Django, derive a class that represents the feed from the `Feed` base class, and define the properties of the feed (title, link, description) and a method called `items` that returns the items of the feed in this class.

- To customize the rendering of item fields in the feed (such as title and description), create a directory called `feeds` in the `templates` directory. Inside it, create templates with filenames that use the format `feedname_fieldname.html`. The contents of these templates will be used to render item fields.

- `Q` objects are very useful to construct complex queries. They encapsulate a filtering condition, and can be combined using `&` ("and"), `|` ("or"), and parentheses.

- Django supports pagination by providing a class named `Paginator`. This class offers various attributes and methods to paginate a query set into multiple pages. Using pagination is highly recommended with large query sets because it improves performance and usability.

In the next chapter, we will build an exciting feature—user networks—that makes our application more social. We will let users invite their friends to join their network and share bookmarks together.

10
Building User Networks

Our application is about "social" bookmarking. Running a social web application means having a community of users who have common interests, and who use the application to share their interests and findings with each other. We will want to enhance the social experience of our users. In this chapter we will introduce two features that will enable us to do this. We will let our users maintain lists of friends, see what their friends are bookmarking, and invite new friends to try out our application. We will also utilize a Django API to make our application more user-friendly and responsive by displaying feedback messages to users. So let's get started!

In this chapter you will learn how to:

- Build a friend network feature
- Let users browse bookmarks of friends
- Enable users to invite friends to your web site
- Improve the interface with status messages

Building friend networks

An important aspect of socializing in our application is letting users to maintain their friend lists and browse through the bookmarks of their friends. So, in this section we will build a data model to maintain user relationships, and then program two views to enable users to manage their friends and browse their friends' bookmarks.

Creating the friendship data model

Let's start with the data model for the friends feature. When a user adds another user as a friend, we need to maintain both users in one object. Therefore, the Friendship data model will consist of two references to the User objects involved in the friendship. Create this model by opening the bookmarks/models.py file and inserting the following code in it:

```
class Friendship(models.Model):
  from_friend = models.ForeignKey(
    User, related_name='friend_set'
  )
  to_friend = models.ForeignKey(
    User, related_name='to_friend_set'
  )
  def __unicode__(self):
    return u'%s, %s' % (
      self.from_friend.username,
      self.to_friend.username
    )
  class Meta:
    unique_together = (('to_friend', 'from_friend'), )
```

The Friendship data model starts with defining two fields that are User objects: from_friend and to_friend. from_friend is the user who added to_friend as a friend. As you can see, we passed a keyword argument called related_name to both the fields. The reason for this is that both fields are foreign keys that refer back to the User data model. This will cause Django to try to create two attributes called friendship_set in each User object, which would result in a name conflict. To avoid this problem, we provide a specific name for each attribute. Consequently, each User object will contain two new attributes: user.friend_set, which contains the friends of this user and user.to_friend_set, which contains the users who added this user as a friend. Throughout this chapter, we will only use the friend_set attribute, but the other one is there in case you need it.

Next, we defined a __unicode__ method in our data model. As you already know, this method is useful for debugging.

Finally, we defined a class called Meta. This class may be used to specify various options related to the data model. Some of the commonly used options are:

- db_table: This is the name of the table to use for the model. This is useful when the table name generated by Django is a reserved keyword in SQL, or when you want to avoid conflicts if a table with the same name already exists in the database.

- ordering: This is a list of field names. It declares how objects are ordered when retrieving a list of objects. A column name may be preceded by a minus sign to change the sorting order from ascending to descending.

- permissions: This lets you declare custom permissions for the data model in addition to add, change, and delete permissions that we learned about in Chapter 7. Permissions should be a list of two-tuples, where each two-tuple should consist of a permission codename and a human-readable name for that permission. For example, you can define a new permission for listing friend bookmarks by using the following Meta class:

```
class Meta:
    permissions = (
        ('can_list_friend_bookmarks',
         'Can list friend bookmarks'),
    )
```

- unique_together: A list of field names that must be unique together.

We used the unique_together option here to ensure that a Friendship object is added only once for a particular relationship. There cannot be two Friendship objects with equal to_friend and from_friend fields. This is equivalent to the following SQL declaration:

```
UNIQUE ("from_friend", "to_friend")
```

If you check the SQL generated by Django for this model, you will find something similar to this in the code.

After entering the data model code into the bookmarks/models.py file, run the following command to create its corresponding table in the database:

```
$ python manage.py syncdb
```

Now let's experiment with the new model and see how to store and retrieve relations of friendship. Run the interactive console using the following command:

```
$ python manage.py shell
```

Next, retrieve some User objects and build relationships between them (but make sure that you have at least three users in the database):

```
>>> from bookmarks.models import *
>>> from django.contrib.auth.models import User
>>> user1 = User.objects.get(id=1)
>>> user2 = User.objects.get(id=2)
>>> user3 = User.objects.get(id=3)
```

```
>>> friendship1 = Friendship(from_friend=user1, to_friend=user2)
>>> friendship1.save()
>>> friendship2 = Friendship(from_friend=user1, to_friend=user3)
>>> friendship2.save()
```

Now, user2 and user3 are both friends of user1. To retrieve the list of Friendship objects associated with user1, use:

```
>>> user1.friend_set.all()

[<Friendship: user1, user2>, <Friendship: user1, user3>]
```

(The actual usernames in output were replaced with user1, user2, and user3 for clarity.)

As you may have already noticed, the attribute is named friend_set because we called it so using the related_name option when we created the Friendship model.

Next, let's see one way to retrieve the User objects of user1's friends:

```
>>> [friendship.to_friend for friendship in
     user1.friend_set.all()]

    [<User: user2>, <User: user3>]
```

The last line of code uses a Python feature called "list" comprehension to build the list of User objects. This feature allows us to build a list by iterating through another list. Here, we built the User list by iterating over a list of Friendship objects. If this syntax looks unfamiliar, please refer to the *List Comprehension* section in the Python tutorial.

Notice that user1 has user2 as a friend, but the opposite is not true.

```
>>> user2.friend_set.all()

    []
```

In other words, the Friendship model works only in one direction. To add user1 as a friend of user2, we need to construct another Friendship object.

```
>>> friendship3 = Friendship(from_friend=user2, to_friend=user1)
>>> friendship3.save()
>>> user2.friend_set.all()

    [<Friendship: user2, user1>]
```

By reversing the arguments passed to the Friendship constructor, we built a relationship in the other way. Now user1 is a friend of user2 and vice-versa.

Experiment more with the model to make sure that you understand how it works. Once you feel comfortable with it, move to the next section, where we will write views to utilize the data model. Things will only get more exciting from now on!

Writing views to manage friends

Now that we are able to store and retrieve user relationships, it's time to create views for these features. In this section we will build two views: one for adding a friend, and another for listing friends and their bookmarks.

We will use the following URL scheme for friend-related views:

- If the view is for managing friends (adding a friend, removing a friend, and so on), its URL should start with /friend/. For example, the URL of the view that adds a friend will be /friend/add/.

- If the view is for viewing friends and their bookmarks, its URL should start with /friends/. For example, /friends/username/ will be used to display the friends of username.

This convention is necessary to avoid conflicts. If we use the prefix /friend/ for all views, what happens if a user registers the username add? The Friends page for this user will be /friend/add/, just like the view to add a friend. The first URL mapping in the URL table will always be used, and the second will become inaccessible, which is obviously a bug.

Now that we have a URL scheme in mind, let's start with writing the friends list view.

The friends list view

This view will receive a username in the URL, and will display this user's friends and their bookmarks. To create the view, open the bookmarks/views.py file and add the following code to it:

```
def friends_page(request, username):
  user = get_object_or_404(User, username=username)
  friends = [friendship.to_friend
             for friendship in user.friend_set.all()]
  friend_bookmarks = Bookmark.objects.filter(
    user__in=friends
  ).order_by('-id')
  variables = RequestContext(request, {
    'username': username,
    'friends': friends,
```

```
        'bookmarks': friend_bookmarks[:10],
        'show_tags': True,
        'show_user': True
    })
    return render_to_response('friends_page.html', variables)
```

This view is pretty simple. It receives a username and operates upon it as follows:

- The `User` object that corresponds to the username is retrieved using the shortcut method `get_object_or_404`.

- The friends of this user are retrieved using the list comprehension syntax mentioned in the previous section.

- After that, the bookmarks of the user's friends are retrieved using the filter method. The `user__in` keyword argument is passed to `filter` in order to retrieve all the bookmarks of the user who exists in the friends list. `order_by` is chained to `filter` for the purpose of sorting bookmarks by `id` in a descending order.

- Finally, the variables are put into a `RequestContext` object and are sent to a template named `friends_page.html`. We used the index syntax with `friend_bookmarks` to get only the latest ten bookmarks.

Let's write the view's template next. Create a file called `friends_page.html` in the `templates` folder with the following code in it:

```
{% extends "base.html" %}

{% block title %}Friends for {{ username }}{% endblock %}
{% block head %}Friends for {{ username }}{% endblock %}

{% block content %}
  <h2>Friend List</h2>
  {% if friends %}
    <ul class="friends">
      {% for friend in friends %}
        <li><a href="/user/{{ friend.username }}/">
          {{ friend.username }}</a></li>
      {% endfor %}
    </ul>
  {% else %}
    <p>No friends found.</p>
  {% endif %}

  <h2>Latest Friend Bookmarks</h2>
  {% include "bookmark_list.html" %}
{% endblock %}
```

The template should be self-explanatory; there is nothing new in it. We iterate over the `friends` list and create a link for each friend. Next, we create a list of friend bookmarks by including the `bookmark_list.html` template.

Finally, we will add a URL entry for the view. Open the `urls.py` file and insert the following mapping into the `urlpatterns` list:

```
urlpatterns = patterns('',
  [...]
  # Friends
  (r'^friends/(\w+)/$', friends_page),
)
```

This URL entry captures the username portion in the URL using a regular expression, exactly the way we did in the `user_page` view.

Although we haven't created a view for adding friends yet, you can still see this view by manually adding some friends to your account (if you haven't done so already). Use the interactive console to make sure that your account has friends, and then start the development server and point your browser to `http://127.0.0.1:8000/friends/your_username/` (replacing `your_username` with your actual username). The resulting page will look something similar to the following screenshot:

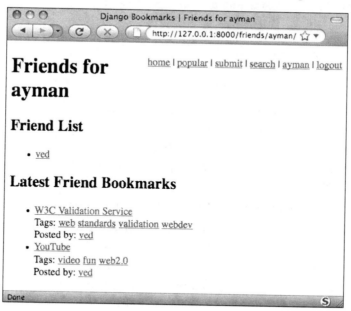

So, we now have a functional Friends page. It displays a list of friends along with their latest bookmarks. In the next section, we are going to create a view that allows users to add friends to this page.

Creating the add friend view

So far, we have been adding friends using the interactive console. The next step in building the friends feature is offering a way to add friends from within our web application.

The `friend_add` view works like this: It receives the username of the friend in GET, and creates a `Friendship` object accordingly. Open the `bookmarks/views.py` file and add the following view:

```
@login_required
def friend_add(request):
  if 'username' in request.GET:
    friend = get_object_or_404(
      User, username=request.GET['username']
    )
    friendship = Friendship(
      from_friend=request.user,
      to_friend=friend
    )
    friendship.save()
    return HttpResponseRedirect(
      '/friends/%s/' % request.user.username
    )
  else:
    raise Http404
```

Let's go through the view line by line:

- We apply the `login_required` decorator to the view. Anonymous users must log in before they can add friends.
- We check whether a GET variable called `username` exists. If it does, we continue with creating a relationship. Otherwise, we raise a 404 page not found error.
- We retrieve the user to be added as a friend using `get_object_or_404`.
- We create a `Friendship` object with the currently logged-in user as the `from_friend` argument, and the requested username as the `to_friend` argument.
- Finally, we redirect the user to their Friends page.

After creating the view, we will add a URL entry for it. Open the `urls.py` file and add the highlighted line to it:

```
urlpatterns = patterns('',
  [...]
  # Friends
  (r'^friends/(\w+)/$', friends_page),
  (r'^friend/add/$', friend_add),
)
```

The "add friend" view is now functional. However, there are no links to use it anywhere in our application, so let's add these links. We will modify the `user_page` view to display a link for adding the current user as a friend, and a link for viewing the user's friends. Of course, we will need to handle special cases; you don't want an "add friend" link when you are viewing your own page, or when you are viewing the page of one of your friends.

Adding these links will be done in the `user_page.html` template. But before doing so, we need to pass a Boolean flag from the `user_page` view to the template indicating whether the owner of the user page is a friend of the currently logged-in user or not. So open the `bookmarks/views.py` file and add the highlighted lines into the `user_page` view:

```
def user_page(request, username):
    user = get_object_or_404(User, username=username)
    query_set = user.bookmark_set.order_by('-id')
    paginator = Paginator(query_set, ITEMS_PER_PAGE)
    if request.user.is_authenticated():
        is_friend = Friendship.objects.filter(
            from_friend=request.user,
            to_friend=user
        )
    else:
        is_friend = False
    try:
        page_number = int(request.GET['page'])
    except (KeyError, ValueError):
        page_number = 1
    try:
        page = paginator.page(page_number)
    except InvalidPage:
        raise Http404
    bookmarks = page.object_list
    variables = RequestContext(request, {
```

```
            'username': username,
            'bookmarks': bookmarks,
            'show_tags': True,
            'show_edit': username == request.user.username,
            'show_paginator': paginator.num_pages > 1,
            'has_prev': page.has_previous(),
            'has_next': page.has_next(),
            'page': page_number,
            'pages': paginator.num_pages,
            'next_page': page_number + 1,
            'prev_page': page_number - 1,
            'is_friend': is_friend,
    })
    return render_to_response('user_page.html', variables)
```

Next, open the `templates/user_page.html` file and add the following highlighted lines to it:

```
[...]
{% block content %}
  {% ifequal user.username username %}
    <a href="/friends/{{ username }}/">view your friends</a>
  {% else %}
    {% if is_friend %}
      <a href="/friends/{{ user.username }}/">
        {{ username }} is a friend of yours</a>
    {% else %}
      <a href="/friend/add/?username={{ username }}">
        add {{ username }} to your friends</a>
    {% endif %}
    - <a href="/friends/{{ username }}/">
        view {{username }}'s friends</a>
  {% endifequal %}
  {% include "bookmark_list.html" %}
{% endblock %}
```

Let's go through each conditional branch in the highlighted code:

1. We check whether the user is viewing his or her page. This is done using a template tag called `ifequal`, which takes two variables to compare for equality. If the user is indeed viewing his or her page, we simply display a link to it.

2. We check whether the user is viewing the page of one of their friends. If this is the case, we display a link to the current user's Friends page instead of an "add friend" link. Otherwise, we construct an "add friend" link by passing the username as a GET variable.

3. We display a link to the Friends page of the user page's owner being viewed.

And that's it. Browse some user pages to see how the links at the top change, depending on your relationship with the owner of the user page. Try to add new friends to see your Friends page grow.

Implementing the friends feature wasn't that hard, was it? You wrote one data model and two views, and the feature became functional. Interestingly, the more Django experience you gain, the more easy and fast its implementation becomes.

Our users are now able to add each other as friends and monitor their friends' bookmarks, but what about friends who are not members of our site? In the next section we will implement an " Invite a friend " feature that will allow users to invite their friends to join our site via email.

Inviting friends via email

Enabling our users to invite their friends carries many benefits. People are more likely to join our site if their friends are already using it. After they join, they will also invite their friends, and so on, which means an increasing number of users for our application. Therefore, it is a good idea to offer an " Invite a friend " feature. This is actually a common functionality found in many Web 2.0 applications.

Building this feature requires the following components:

- An `Invitation` data model to store invitations in the database
- A form in which users can type the emails of their friends and send invitations
- An invitation email with an activation link
- A mechanism for processing activation links sent in email

Throughout this section, we will implement each component. But because this section involves sending emails, we first need to configure Django to send emails by adding some options to the `settings.py` file. So, open the `settings.py` file and add the following lines to it:

```
SITE_HOST = '127.0.0.1:8000'
DEFAULT_FROM_EMAIL = \
    'Django Bookmarks <django.bookmarks@example.com>'
EMAIL_HOST = 'mail.yourisp.com'
EMAIL_PORT = ''
EMAIL_HOST_USER = 'username'
EMAIL_HOST_PASSWORD = 'password'
```

Let's see what each variable does.

- SITE_HOST: This is the host name of your server. Leave it as 127.0.0.1:8000 for now. When we deploy our server in the next chapter, we will change this.

- DEFAULT_FROM_EMAIL: This is the email address that appears in the **From** field of emails sent by Django.

- EMAIL_HOST: This is the host name of your email server. If you are using a development machine that doesn't run a mail server (which is most likely the case), then you need to put your ISP's outgoing email server here. Contact your ISP for more information.

- EMAIL_PORT: This refers to the port number of the outgoing email server. If you leave it empty, the default value (25) will be used. You also need to obtain this from your ISP.

- EMAIL_HOST_USER and EMAIL_HOST_PASSWORD: This refers to the username and password for the outgoing email server. For the host username, input your username and your email server (as shown in the previous code). Leave the fields empty if your ISP does not require them.

To verify that your settings are correct, launch the interactive shell and enter the following:

```
>>> from django.core.mail import send_mail
>>> send_mail('Subject', 'Body of the message.',
            'from@example.com',
            ['your_email@example.com'])
```

Replace your_email@example.com with your actual email address. If the above call to send_mail does not raise an exception and you receive the email, then all is set. Otherwise, you need to verify your settings with your ISP and try again.

Once the settings are correct, sending an email in Django is a piece of cake! We will use send_mail to send the invitation email. But first, let's create a data model for storing invitations.

The invitation data model

An invitation consists of the following information:

- Recipient name
- Recipient email
- The User object of the sender

We also need to store an activation code for the invitation. This code will be sent in the invitation email. The code will serve two purposes:

- Before accepting the invitation, we can use the code to verify that the invitation actually exists in the database
- After accepting the invitation, we can use the code to retrieve the invitation information from the database and create friendship relationships between the sender and the recipient

With this in mind, let's create the `Invitation` data model. Open the `bookmarks/models.py` file and append the following code to it:

```
class Invitation(models.Model):
  name = models.CharField(max_length=50)
  email = models.EmailField()
  code = models.CharField(max_length=20)
  sender = models.ForeignKey(User)

  def __unicode__(self):
    return u'%s, %s' % (self.sender.username, self.email)
```

There shouldn't be anything new or difficult to understand in this model. We simply defined fields for the recipient name, recipient email, activation code, and the sender of the invitation. We also created a `__unicode__` method for debugging, and enabled the model in the administration interface. Do not forget to run `manage.py syncdb` to create the new model's table in the database.

Next, we will add a method for sending the invitation email. The method will use classes and methods from several packages. So, put the following `import` statements at the beginning of the `bookmarks/models.py` file, and append the `send` method to the `Invitation` data model in the same file:

```
from django.core.mail import send_mail
from django.template.loader import get_template
from django.template import Context
from django.conf import settings
class Invitation(models.Model):
  [...]
  def send(self):
    subject = u'Invitation to join Django Bookmarks'
    link = 'http://%s/friend/accept/%s/' % (
      settings.SITE_HOST,
      self.code
    )
    template = get_template('invitation_email.txt')
    context = Context({
```

```
      'name': self.name,
      'link': link,
      'sender': self.sender.username,
    })
    message = template.render(context)
    send_mail(
      subject, message,
      settings.DEFAULT_FROM_EMAIL, [self.email]
    )
```

The method works by loading a template called `invitation_email.txt` and passing the following variables to it: the name of the recipient, the activation link, and the sender username. The template is then used to render the body of the invitation email. After that, we used `send_mail` to send the email as we did during the interactive session in the previous section.

There are several observations to make here:

- The format of the activation link is `http://SITE_HOST/friend/accept/CODE/`. We will write a view to handle such URLs later in this section.

- This is the first time we use a template to render something other than a web page. As you can see, the template system is quite flexible and allows us to build emails as well as web pages, or any other text.

- We used the `get_template` and `render` methods to build the message body as opposed to the usual `render_to_response` call. If you remember, this is how we rendered templates early in the book. We are doing this here because we are not rendering a web page.

- The last parameter of `send_mail` is a list of recipient emails. Here we are passing only one email address. But if you want to send the same email to multiple users, you can pass all of the email addresses in one list to `send_mail`.

Since the `send` method loads a template called `invitation_email.txt`, create a file with this name in the `templates` folder and insert the following content into it:

```
Hi {{ name }},
{{ sender }} invited you to join Django Bookmarks,
  a website where you can post and share your bookmarks with friends!
To accept the invitation, please click the link below:
{{ link }}
-- Django Bookmarks Team
```

Once we write the `send` method, our `Invitation` data model is ready. Next, we will create a form that allows users to send invitations.

The Invite A Friend form and view

The next step in implementing the " Invite a friend " feature is providing users with a form to enter their friends' details and invite them. We will create this form now. The task will be quite similar to compiling the forms that we have built throughout this book.

First, let's create a `Form` class that represents our form. Open the `bookmarks/forms.py` file and add this class to it:

```
class FriendInviteForm(forms.Form):
  name = forms.CharField(label=u'Friend\'s Name')
  email = forms.EmailField(label=u'Friend\'s Email')
```

This form is simple. We only ask the user to enter the friend's name and email. Let's create a view to display and handle this form. Open the `bookmarks/views.py` file and append the following code to it:

```
@login_required
def friend_invite(request):
  if request.method == 'POST':
    form = FriendInviteForm(request.POST)
    if form.is_valid():
      invitation = Invitation(
        name=form.cleaned_data['name'],
        email=form.cleaned_data['email'],
        code=User.objects.make_random_password(20),
        sender=request.user
      )
      invitation.save()
      invitation.send()
      return HttpResponseRedirect('/friend/invite/')
  else:
    form = FriendInviteForm()

  variables = RequestContext(request, {
    'form': form
  })
  return render_to_response('friend_invite.html', variables)
```

Again, the view is similar to the other form processing views in our application. If a valid form is submitted, it creates an `Invitation` object and sends it. We used a method called `make_random_password` in `User.objects` to generate an activation code for the invitation. This method can be used to create random passwords. It takes the length of the password as a parameter and returns a random alphanumeric password.

After this, we will add a template for the view. Create a file called `friend_invite.html` in the `templates` folder with the following code:

```
{% extends "base.html" %}
{% block title %}Invite A Friend{% endblock %}
{% block head %}Invite A Friend{% endblock %}
{% block content %}
Enter your friend name and email below,
and click "send invite" to invite your friend to join the site:
<form method="post" action=".">
  {{ form.as_p }}
  <input type="submit" value="send invite" />
</form>
{% endblock %}
```

As you can see, the template displays a help message and the form below it.

Finally, we will add a URL entry for this view, so open the `urls.py` file and add the highlighted line to it:

```
urlpatterns = patterns('',
  [...]
  # Friends
  (r'^friends/(\w+)/$', friends_page),
  (r'^friend/add/$', friend_add),
  (r'^friend/invite/$', friend_invite),
)
```

The **Invite A Friend** view is now ready. Open `http://127.0.0.1:8000/friend/invite/` in your browser, and you will see a form similar to the following screenshot:

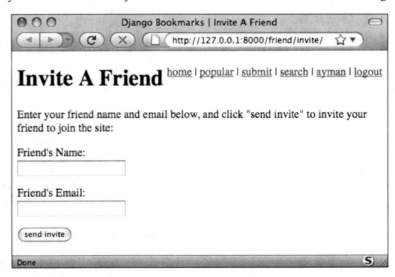

Try to send an invitation to your email address. If everything is working correctly, you will receive an invitation with an activation link similar to the following screenshot:

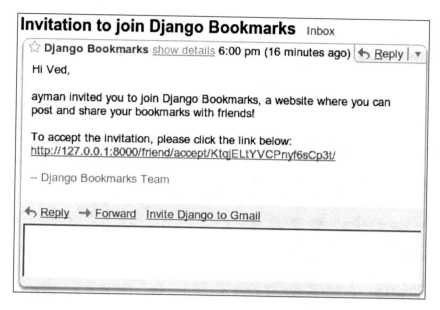

We are half-way through implementing the " Invite a friend " feature. At the moment, clicking the activation link produces a 404 page not found error. So we will now write a view to handle it.

Handling activation links

We have made good progress; users are now able to send invitations to their friends via email. The next step is building a mechanism for handling activation links in invitations. Here is an outline of what we are going to do:

- We will build a view that handles activation links. This view verifies that the invitation code actually exists in the database, stores the invitation ID in the user's session, and redirects to the registration page.

- When the user registers an account, we check to see if they have an invitation ID in their session. If this is the case, we retrieve the Invitation object for this ID, and build friendship relationships between the user and the sender of the invitation.

Let's start by writing a URL entry for the view. Open the urls.py file and add the highlighted line from the following code to it:

```
urlpatterns = patterns('',
  [...]
  # Friends
  (r'^friends/(\w+)/$', friends_page),
  (r'^friend/add/$', friend_add),
  (r'^friend/invite/$', friend_invite),
  (r'^friend/accept/(\w+)/$', friend_accept),
)
```

As you can see, the view follows the URL format sent in invitation emails. The activation code is captured from the URL using a regular expression, and then it will be passed to the view as a parameter. Next, we will write the view. Open the bookmarks/views.py file and create the following view in it:

```
def friend_accept(request, code):
    invitation = get_object_or_404(Invitation, code__exact=code)
    request.session['invitation'] = invitation.id
    return HttpResponseRedirect('/register/')
```

The view is short and concise. It tries to retrieve the Invitation object that corresponds to the requested code (generating a 404 error if the code does not exist). After that, it stores the ID of the object in the user's session. Lastly, it redirects to the registration page.

This is the first time that we use sessions in our application. Django provides an easy-to-use session framework to store and retrieve data for each visitor. Data is stored on the server and can be accessed in views by using a dictionary-like object available at request.session.

The session framework is enabled by default in the settings.py file. You can verify this by looking for 'django.contrib.sessions' in the INSTALLED_APPS variable.

You can use request.session to do the following:

- Store a key-value pair: request.session[key] = value
- Retrieve a value by providing its key: value = request.session[key]. This raises KeyError if the key does not exist.
- Check whether the session contains a particular key:
  if key in request.session:

Each user has its own session dictionary. Sessions are useful for maintaining data across requests, especially for anonymous users. Unlike cookies, sessions are stored on the server side so that they cannot be tampered with.

All of these properties make sessions ideal for passing the invitation ID to the register_page view. After this quick overview of the session framework, let's get back to our current task. Now that the friend_accept view is ready, we will modify the register_page view a little to make use of the invitation ID in the user's session. If the ID exists, we will create friendship relations between the user and the sender, and delete the invitation to prevent reusing it. Open the bookmarks/views.py file and add the highlighted lines from the following code:

```python
def register_page(request):
  if request.method == 'POST':
    form = RegistrationForm(request.POST)
    if form.is_valid():
      user = User.objects.create_user(
        username=form.cleaned_data['username'],
        password=form.cleaned_data['password1'],
        email=form.cleaned_data['email']
      )
      if 'invitation' in request.session:
        # Retrieve the invitation object.
        invitation = Invitation.objects.get(
          id=request.session['invitation']
        )
        # Create friendship from user to sender.
        friendship = Friendship(
          from_friend=user,
          to_friend=invitation.sender
        )
        friendship.save()
        # Create friendship from sender to user.
        friendship = Friendship (
          from_friend=invitation.sender,
          to_friend=user
        )
        friendship.save()
        # Delete the invitation from the database and session.
        invitation.delete()
        del request.session['invitation']
      return HttpResponseRedirect('/register/success/')
```

```
else:
    form = RegistrationForm()
variables = RequestContext(request, {
    'form': form
})
return render_to_response('registration/register.html', variables)
```

The highlighted code should be easy to understand. It starts by checking for an invitation ID in the user's session. If there is one, it creates the relation of friendship in both directions between the sender of the invitation and the current user. After that, it deletes the invitation and removes its ID from the session.

Feel free to create a link to the Invite A Friend page. The Friends list page is a good place to do so. Open the `templates/friends_page.html` file and add the highlighted line from the following code:

```
{% extends "base.html" %}
{% block title %}Friends for {{ username }}{% endblock %}
{% block head %}Friends for {{ username }}{% endblock %}
{% block content %}
  <h2>Friend List</h2>
  {% if friends %}
    <ul class="friends">
      {% for friend in friends %}
        <li><a href="/user/{{ friend.username }}/">
          {{ friend.username }}</a></li>
      {% endfor %}
    </ul>
  {% else %}
    <p>No friends found.</p>
  {% endif %}
  <a href="/friend/invite/">Invite a friend!</a>
  <h2>Latest Friend Bookmarks</h2>
  {% include 'bookmark_list.html' %}
{% endblock %}
```

This should be all that we need to do to implement the " Invite a friend " feature. It was a bit long, but we were able to put various areas of our Django knowledge to good use while implementing it. You can now click on the invitation link that you received via email to see what happens—you will be redirected to the registration page. Create a new account there, log in, and notice how the new account and your original one have become friends with each other.

Improving the interface with messages

Although our implementation of user networks is working correctly, there is something missing. The interface does not tell the user whether an operation succeeded or failed. After sending an invitation, for example, the user is redirected back to the invitation form, with no feedback on whether the operation was successful or not. In this section, we are going to improve our interface by providing status messages to the user after performing certain actions.

Displaying messages to users is done using the message API, which is part of the authentication system. The API is simple. To create a message, you can use the following call:

```
request.user.message_set.create(
  message=u'Message text goes here.'
)
```

This call will create a message and store it in the database. Available messages are accessible from within templates through the variable messages. The following code iterates over messages and displays them in a list:

```
{% if messages %}
<ul>
    {% for message in messages %}
      <li>{{ message }}</li>
    {% endfor %}
</ul>
{% endif %}
```

This information covers all that we need to utilize the message framework in our project. Let's start by placing the above template code in the base template of our application. Open the templates/base.html file and add the highlighted section of the following code:

```
<body>
  <div id="nav">
     [...]
  </div>
  <h1>{% block head %}{% endblock %}</h1>
  {% if messages %}
    <ul class="messages">
      {% for message in messages %}
        <li>{{ message }}</li>
      {% endfor %}
    </ul>
  {% endif %}
  {% block content %}{% endblock %}
</body>
</html>
```

We placed the code below the heading of the page. To give messages a distinctive look, add the following CSS code to the `site_media/style.css` file:

```css
ul.messages {
  border: 1px dashed #000;
  margin: 1em 4em;
  padding: 1em;
}
```

And that's about it. We can now create messages and they will be displayed automatically. Let's start with sending invitations. Open the `bookmarks/views.py` files and modify the `friend_invite` view as follows:

```python
import smtplib

@login_required
def friend_invite(request):
    if request.method == 'POST':
        form = FriendInviteForm(request.POST)
        if form.is_valid():
            invitation = Invitation(
                name=form.cleaned_data['name'],
                email=form.cleaned_data['email'],
                code=User.objects.make_random_password(20),
                sender=request.user
            )
            invitation.save()
            try:
                invitation.send()
                request.user.message_set.create(
                    message=u'An invitation was sent to %s.' %
                        invitation.email
                )
            except smtplib.SMTPException:
                request.user.message_set.create(
                    message=u'An error happened when '
                        u'sending the invitation.'
                )
            return HttpResponseRedirect('/friend/invite/')
    else:
        form = FriendInviteForm()
    variables = RequestContext(request, {
        'form': form
    })
    return render_to_response('friend_invite.html', variables)
```

The highlighted code works as follows: `send_mail` raises an exception if it fails, so we wrap the call to `invitation.send` in a `try/except` block. The reader is then notified accordingly.

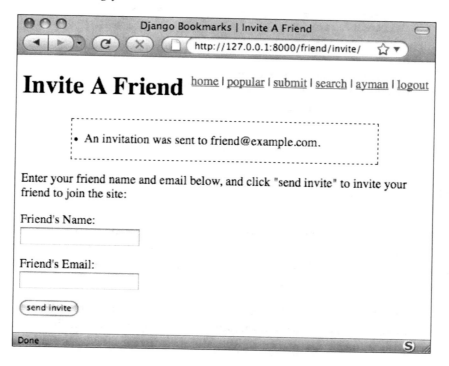

You can try the new message system now. First, send an invitation and notice how a message appears confirming the success of the operation. Next, change the `EMAIL_HOST` option in the `settings.py` file to an invalid value and try sending an invitation again. You should see a message indicating failure this time. Our interface is more responsive now. Users know exactly what's going on.

You can do the same for the `friend_add` view. Open the `bookmarks/views.py` file and modify the view like this:

```
@login_required
def friend_add(request):
    if 'username' in request.GET:
        friend = get_object_or_404(
            User, username=request.GET['username']
        )
        friendship = Friendship(
            from_friend=request.user,
            to_friend=friend
        )
```

```
  try:
    friendship.save()
    request.user.message_set.create(
      message=u'%s was added to your friend list.' %
        friend.username
    )
  except:
    request.user.message_set.create(
      message=u'%s is already a friend of yours.' %
        friend.username
)
  return HttpResponseRedirect(
    '/friends/%s/' % request.user.username
  )
else:
  raise Http404
```

The highlighted code displays a success message if the call to `friendship.save` was successful. If an exception is thrown by the call, it means that the `unique_together` condition was violated and that the requested username is already a friend of the current user. An error message that says so is displayed.

The message API is simple, yet effective. You can use it for all sorts of things, such as displaying status messages, errors, notifications, and so on. Try to utilize it in other parts of the application if you want, such as after adding or editing a bookmark.

Summary

We developed an important set of features for our project in this chapter. Friend networks are very important in helping users to socialize and share interests together. These features are common in Web 2.0 applications, and now you are able to incorporate them into any Django web site.

Here is a quick summary of the Django features covered in this chapter:

- To manually specify a name for the related attribute in a data model, pass a keyword argument called `related_name` to the field that creates the relationship between models.

- You can specify several options for data models by defining a class called `Meta` inside the data model. Some of the possible attributes in this class are: `db_table`, `ordering`, `permissions`, and `unique_together`.

- To send an email in Django, use the `send_mail` function. It's available from the `django.core.mail` package.

- The Django session framework provides a convenient way to store and retrieve user data across requests. The `request.session` object provides a dictionary-like interface to interact with session data.

- To create a message, use the following method call:
  `request.user.message_set.create`.

- To display messages in a template, use the template variable `messages`.

In the next chapter we will learn about improving various aspects of our application— mainly, performance and localization. We will also learn how to deploy our project on a production server. The next chapter comes with a lot of useful information, so keep reading!

11
Extending and Deploying

In this chapter, we will prepare the social bookmarking application for deployment into production by utilizing various Django frameworks. We will add support for multiple languages, improve performance by caching, automate testing, and configure the project for a production environment. This chapter has a lot of interesting and useful information, so make sure you go through it before publishing your application online!

In this chapter you will learn about the following:

- Internationalization: Offering your site in multiple languages
- Caching: Improving the performance of your site during high traffic
- Unit testing: Automating the process of testing your application
- Deployment: Configuring your web site for a production environment

Internationalization (i18n)

People won't use our application if they cannot read its pages. So far, we have been concerned with English-speaking users only. However, there are people all over the world who do not know English, or prefer to use their native language. To appeal to those people, it would be a good idea to offer the interface of our application in multiple languages. This would overcome the language barrier and open new frontiers for our application, especially in regions where English knowledge is not common.

As you may have guessed, Django provides all of the components needed to translate a project into multiple languages. The system that is responsible for providing this feature is called the **internationalization system** (i18n for short). The process of translating a Django project is quite simple. You basically follow these three steps:

- Specify what strings should be translated in your application. For example, status and error messages are translatable, whereas usernames are not.

- Create a translation file for each language that you want to support.
- Enable and configure the i18n system.

In the subsections that follow, we will go through each step in detail. By the end of this section, our application will support multiple languages, and you will be able to translate any other Django project with ease.

Marking strings as translatable

The first step in translating an application is telling Django what strings should be translated. Generally speaking, strings that are a part of views and templates need to be translated, while strings that are entered by the user do not need to be. A string can be marked as translatable with a function call. The name of the function and how it is called depends on whether the string is located in a view, template, model, or form.

This step is much easier than it initially looks. Let's learn about it through an example. We will translate the "invite friend" functionality in our application. The process of translating the rest of the application will be exactly the same. Open the bookmarks/views.py file and make the highlighted changes to the friend_invite view:

```
from django.utils.translation import ugettext as _
@login_required
def friend_invite(request):
  if request.method == 'POST':
    form = FriendInviteForm(request.POST)
    if form.is_valid():
      invitation = Invitation(
        name=form.cleaned_data['name'],
        email=form.cleaned_data['email'],
        code=User.objects.make_random_password(20),
        sender=request.user
      )
      invitation.save()
      try:
        invitation.send()
        request.user.message_set.create(
          message=_(u'An invitation was sent to %s.') %
            invitation.email
        )
      except smtplib.SMTPException:
        request.user.message_set.create(
          message=_(u'An error happened when '
            u'sending the invitation.')
```

```
      )
        return HttpResponseRedirect('/friend/invite/')
      else:
        form = FriendInviteForm()
      variables = RequestContext(request, {
        'form': form
      })
      return render_to_response('friend_invite.html', variables)
```

As you can see, the changes are minimal:

- We imported a function called ugettext from django.utils.translation.

- We used the as keyword to assign a shorter name to the function (_ the underscore character). We did so because this function will be used to mark strings as translatable in views. Since this is a very common task, it's a good idea to give the function a shorter name.

- We marked a string as translatable simply by passing it to the _ function.

That was pretty simple, wasn't it? There is one little observation to make here. The first message uses string formatting, and we applied the % operator after calling the _ function. This is necessary to avoid translating the email address. It's also preferable to use named formats, which gives greater control while doing the actual translation later. So you may want to do something like this:

```
message= _('An invitation was sent to %(email)s.') %
  {'email': invitation.email}
```

Now that we know how to mark strings as translatable in views, let's move to templates. Open the friend_invite.html file in the templates folder and modify it as follows:

```
{% extends "base.html" %}
{% load i18n %}
{% block title %}{% trans 'Invite A Friend' %}{% endblock %}
{% block head %}{% trans 'Invite A Friend' %}{% endblock %}
{% block content %}
{% trans 'Enter your friend name and email below, and click
  "send invite" to invite your friend to join the site:' %}
<form method="post" action=".">
  {{ form.as_p }}
  <input type="submit" value="{% trans 'send invite' %}" />
</form>
{% endblock %}
```

Here we placed `{% load i18n %}` at the beginning of the template to give it access to translation tags. The `load` tag is usually used to enable additional template tags that are not available by default. You need to place it near the top of every template that uses translation tags. `i18n` is shorthand for internationalization, which is the name of the Django framework that provides translation features.

Next, we used a template tag called `trans` to mark strings as translatable. This template tag works in exactly the same way as the `ugettext` function in views. It's worth noting that the `trans` tag does not work if the string contains a template variable. In this case, you would need to use the `blocktrans` tag like this:

```
{% blocktrans %}This tag may have a {{ variable }}
    inside.{% endblocktrans %}
```

Now you know how to deal with translatable strings in templates, too. So let's move to forms and models. Marking a string as translatable in a form or model is slightly different from the way this is done in views. To learn how it is done, open the `bookmarks/forms.py` file and modify the `FriendInvite` form like this:

```
from django.utils.translation import ugettext_lazy as _

class FriendInviteForm(forms.Form):
    name = forms.CharField(label=_("Friend's Name"))
    email = forms.EmailField(label=_("Friend's Email"))
```

The only difference here is that we imported `ugettext_lazy` instead of `ugettext`. `ugettext_lazy` delays translating the string until its return value is accessed. This is needed here because the attributes of the form are created only once—when the application is started. If we use the normal `ugettext` function, the translated labels will be stored in the `form` attributes using the default language (usually English) and will never be translated again. However, if we use `ugettext_lazy`, the function will return a special object that will translate the string every time it is accessed. Hence, the translation will be done correctly. This feature makes the `ugettext_lazy` function ideal for the `form` and `model` attributes.

With this, we finish marking the strings of the "invite friend" view for translation. To help you remember what's covered in this subsection, here is a quick summary of the techniques used to mark translatable strings:

- In views, mark translatable strings using the `ugettext` function (usually imported as _)
- In templates, mark translatable strings using the `trans` template tag for strings that do not contain variables, and `blocktrans` for strings that do
- In forms and models, mark translatable strings using the `ugettext_lazy` function (usually imported as _)

Of course, there are special cases that may need to be handled separately. For example, you may want to translate the default parameter values in views using `ugettext_lazy` instead of `ugettext`. As long as you understand the difference between these two functions, you should be able to decide when you need to do so.

Creating translation files

Now that we have finished marking strings for translation, the next step is creating a translation file for each language that we want to support. This file contains all translatable strings along with their translations. It is created using a utility provided by Django.

Let's create a translation file. Django uses a software package called GNU `gettext` to extract translatable strings from a source code, so you need to install this package. For Linux, search for the package in your package manager and install it.

For Windows:

1. Users need to dowload three ZIP files from:

   `http://sourceforge.net/projects/gettext`

   ° `gettext-runtime-X.bin.woe32.zip`

   ° `gettext-tools-X.bin.woe32.zip`

   ° `libiconv-X.bin.woe32.zip`

2. Extract the three files in the same folder (that is, `C:\Program Files\gettext-utils`).

3. Update the system **PATH** :

   Control Panel > System > Advanced > Environment Variables

   In the **System variables** list, click **Path**, click **Edit**.

   Add `;C:\Program Files\gettext-utils\bin` at the end of the **Variable value**.

And finally, Mac OS X users will find a version of the package for their operating system along with installation instructions at:

`http://gettext.darwinports.com/`

Once you have the GNU `gettext` package installed, open a terminal, go to your project directory, create the directory `locale` there, and then run the following command:

```
$ python manage.py makemessages -l de
```

This command creates a translation file for the German language. `de` is the language code for German. If you want to target another language, put its language code instead of `de` and continue to do so during the rest of the chapter. In addition, if you want to support more than one language, run the previous command for each language and apply the instructions in the rest of the section to all languages.

When you run the above command, it will create a file called `django.po` at `locale/de/LC_MESSAGES/`. This is the translation file for the German language. Open it in a text editor to see what it looks like. The file starts with some metadata, such as creation date and character set. After that, you will find an entry for each translatable string. Each entry consists of the filename and the line number of the string, the string itself, and an empty string below it where the translation should go. Here is a sample entry from the file:

```
#: bookmarks/forms.py:62
msgid "Friend's Name"
msgstr ""
```

To translate the string, simply use your text editor to type the translation in the empty string on the third line. You can also use a specialized translation editor, such as **poEdit** (available for all major operating systems at `http://www.poedit.net/`). But for our simple file, a regular text editor should suffice. Make sure you put a valid character set in the meta data section of the file. I recommend using UTF-8.

```
"Content-Type: text/plain; charset=UTF-8\n"
```

You may notice that the translation file contains some strings from the admin interface. This is because the admin template `admin/base_site.html` uses the `trans` template tag to mark its strings as translatable. There is no need to translate these strings — Django already comes with translation files for them.

After translating, you need to compile the translation file into a format that Django can use. This is done by running the following command from within your project command:

```
$ python manage.py compilemessages
```

If the utility complains about an error in the file (such as a missing quotation mark), correct the error and try again. Once successful, the utility will create a compiled translation file called `django.mo` in the same folder, and everything will be set for the next step in this section.

Enabling and configuring the i18n system

By default, Django comes with the i18n system enabled. You can verify this by searching for the following line in the `settings.py` file:

```
USE_I18N = True
```

Django enables a long list of languages by default. In practice, however, your application will only support a subset of these languages. To enable specific languages in your Django application, define a tuple called `LANGUAGES` in the `settings.py` file as follows:

```
LANGUAGES = (
    ('en', 'English'),
    ('de', 'German'),
)
```

There are two ways to configure the i18n system. You can either globally set the language for all users, or let users specify their preferred languages individually. We will look at both the methods in this subsection.

To set the active language globally, find the variable called `LANGUAGE_CODE` in the `settings.py` file and assign your preferred language code to it. For example, if you want to set German as the default language for our project, change the language code as follows:

```
LANGUAGE_CODE = 'de'
```

Now, start the development server if it's not already running, and navigate to the Invite A Friend page. There, you will find that the strings have changed according to what you entered in the German translation file. Change the value of `LANGUAGE_CODE` to `'en'` and notice how the page reverts back to English.

The second configuration method is letting users choose the language. To do so, we should enable a class called `LocaleMiddleware`. To put it simply, a middleware is a class that processes a request or response object. Many components of Django make use of middleware classes to implement features. To see this, open the `settings.py` file and search for `MIDDLEWARE_CLASSES`. You will find a list of strings there. One of them will be `'django.contrib.sessions.middleware.SessionMiddleware'`, which attaches session data to the request object. We don't need to learn how middleware classes are implemented before using them. To enable `LocaleMiddleware`, simply add its class path to the `MIDDLEWARE_CLASSES` list. Make sure you put `LocaleMiddleware` after `SessionMiddleware` because the locale middleware utilizes the session API as we will see next.

Open the `settings.py` file and modify it, as highlighted in the following code:

```
MIDDLEWARE_CLASSES = (
    'django.middleware.common.CommonMiddleware',
    'django.contrib.sessions.middleware.SessionMiddleware',
    'django.contrib.auth.middleware.AuthenticationMiddleware',
    'django.middleware.locale.LocaleMiddleware',
)
```

`LocaleMiddleware` determines the active language for the user by following these steps:

- It looks for a key named `django_language` in session data.
- If the key does not exist, it looks for a cookie called `django_language`.
- If the cookie does not exist, it looks at the language codes in the `Accept-Language` HTTP header. This header is sent by the browser to the web server indicating which languages you would prefer to receive content in.
- If all else fails, the `LANGUAGE_CODE` variable in the `settings.py` file is used.

In all of these steps, Django looks for a language code that matches one of the available translation files. To effectively utilize the locale middleware, we need a view that enables the user to choose a language and updates session data accordingly. Fortunately, Django already comes with such a view for us to use. The view is called `setlanguage` and it expects a language code in a `POST` variable called `language`. It updates session data using this variable, and redirects to the originating page. To enable this view, edit the `urls.py` file and add the highlighted lines shown in the following code:

```
urlpatterns = patterns('',
    [...]
    # i18n
    (r'^i18n/', include('django.conf.urls.i18n')),
)
```

Adding the above line is similar to how we added URL entries for the admin interface. If you recall from a previous chapter, the `include` function can be used to include URL entries from another application under a specific path. Now, we can let the user change the language to German by providing a form that posts a language code to `/i18n/setlang/`. We will modify the base template to add such a form in all the pages. Open the `templates/base.html` file and add the highlighted lines to it:

```
{% load i18n %}
<!DOCTYPE html PUBLIC "-//W3C//DTD XHTML 1.0 Transitional//EN"
    "http://www.w3.org/TR/xhtml1/DTD/xhtml1-transitional.dtd">
```

```
<html>
<head>
  [...]
</head>

<body>
  [...]
  <div id="footer">
    <form action="/i18n/setlang/" method="post">
      <select name="language">
        {% for lang in LANGUAGES %}
          <option value="{{ lang.0 }}">{{ lang.1 }}</option>
        {% endfor %}
      </select>
      <input type="submit" value="Go" />
    </form>
  </div>
</body>
</html>
```

Additionally, we will style the new footer by appending the following CSS code to the `site_media/style.css` file:

```
#footer {
  margin-top: 2em;
  text-align: center;
#footer input {
  display: inline;
}
```

The i18n functionality of our application is now ready. Point your browser to the Invite A Friend page and try the new language links at the bottom. The language should change according to the link clicked.

Before we conclude this section, there are a few observations to make:

- You can access the currently active language in views using the `request.LANGUAGE_CODE` attribute.

- Django itself is translated into a large number of languages. You can see this by triggering a form error when a language other than English is active. Error messages will appear in the selected language even though you didn't translate them yourself.

- In templates, when `RequestContext` is used, the currently active language is accessible using the template variable `LANGUAGE_CODE`.

This section was a bit long, but we learned a very important feature from it. By offering our application in multiple languages, we make it accessible to a broader audience. This gives it a greater potential to attract more and more users. This actually applies to any web application, and now you are able to translate any Django project into multiple languages with ease.

The next section shifts to a different topic. When the user base of your application grows, the load on your server will increase and you will start to look for ways to improve the performance of your application. This is where caching comes to the rescue. So, please read on to learn about this very useful technique.

Improving performance with caching

Pages of web applications are dynamically generated. Code is executed to process user input and generate output every time a page is requested. There are a lot of overheads involved in generating dynamic pages, especially when compared to serving static HTML files. The code may connect to a database, perform computationally expensive calculations, process files, and so on. At the same time, being able to generate pages with code is exactly what makes a web site dynamic and interactive. Wouldn't it be great if we could get the best of both worlds? This is what caching does, and it's a feature that is implemented in most sites with medium to high traffic.

When a page is requested, caching works by storing the generated HTML of the page and reusing it later when the same page is requested again. This cuts a lot of overheads by avoiding the need to generate the same page over and over. Of course, cached pages are not stored forever. When a page is cached, an expiration period is set for the cache. When the cached page expires, it is deleted and the page is generated and cached again. The expiration period is usually between a few seconds and a few minutes, depending on the traffic of the site. The expiration period ensures that the cache is updated periodically, and that users receive content updates. At the same time, it reduces the overhead of generating pages.

Although caching is most useful for medium to high-traffic sites, sites with low traffic can also benefit from it. If the site happens to receive a surge of high traffic suddenly (perhaps because it was featured on a major news site), you can enable caching to reduce the server load and help your web site survive the surge of high traffic. Later when the traffic calms down, you can turn the caching off. So caching is also useful for small web sites. You never know when you may need it, so it's always good to have this information ready.

Enabling caching

We will start this section by enabling the caching system. To use caching, you first need to choose a caching backend and specify your choice in a variable called `CACHE_BACKEND` in the `settings.py` file. The contents of this variable depend on what caching backend you choose. Some of the available options are as follows:

Local memory caching

Cache data is stored in the local memory. This is useful only to test the caching system during development and must not be used in production. To enable it, add the following to the `settings.py` file:

```
CACHE_BACKEND = 'locmem:///'
```

Database caching

Cache data is stored in a database table. To create the cache table, run the following command:

```
$ python manage.py createcachetable cache_table
```

Next, add the following to the `settings.py` file:

```
CACHE_BACKEND = 'db://cache_table'
```

Here the cache table was called `cache_table`. You can call it whatever you want, as long as it doesn't conflict with an existing table.

File system caching

Cache data is stored in the local file system. To use it, add the following to the `settings.py` file:

```
CACHE_BACKEND = 'file:///tmp/django_cache'
```

Here, `/tmp/django_cache` is used to store cache files. You can specify another path if you like. Windows users may want to use `c:\tmp\django_cache`.

Memcached

Memcached is an advanced, highly efficient, and fast caching framework. Installing and configuring it is beyond the scope of this book. But if you already have a Memcached server available, you can specify its IP and port in the `settings.py` file like this:

```
CACHE_BACKEND = 'memcached://ip:port/'
```

If you are not sure what backend to choose for this section, go with the local memory caching. In reality, however, if you are caught in a sudden surge of traffic and want to improve server performance, go with Memcached or database caching, depending on what's available to you on the server. On the other hand, if you have a web site with medium to high traffic, I highly recommend using Memcached because it is definitely the fastest caching solution available for Django. The information presented in this section works the same regardless of what caching backend you choose.

So, decide on a caching backend and insert the corresponding `CACHE_BACKEND` variable in the `settings.py` file. Next, you should specify the expiration duration of cached pages in seconds. Add the following to the `settings.py` file to cache pages for five minutes:

```
CACHE_MIDDLEWARE_SECONDS = 60 * 5
```

We are done with enabling the caching system. Continue reading to learn how to utilize caching to improve the performance of your application.

Configuring caching

You can configure Django to cache your whole site or specific views. We will learn how to do both in this subsection.

Caching the whole site

To cache your whole site, add the following classes to your `MIDDLEWARE_CLASSES` in the `settings.py` file:

```
MIDDLEWARE_CLASSES = (
    'django.middleware.cache.UpdateCacheMiddleware',
    'django.middleware.common.CommonMiddleware',
    'django.contrib.sessions.middleware.SessionMiddleware',
    'django.contrib.auth.middleware.AuthenticationMiddleware',
    'django.middleware.locale.LocaleMiddleware',
    'django.middleware.cache.FetchFromCacheMiddleware',
)
```

Order matters here, as it did when we added the locale middleware. The `UpdateCacheMiddleware` class must be the first, and the `FetchFromCacheMiddleware` class must be the last.

This is all that you need to cache your Django site. From now on, whenever a page is requested, Django will store the generated HTML and re-use it later. It's important to realize that the caching system only caches pages that do not have GET and POST variables. Therefore, our users will still be able to post bookmarks and add friends because the views of these pages expect GET or POST variables. On the other hand, pages such as bookmark and tag listings will be cached.

Caching specific views

Sometimes you will want to cache only specific pages of your web site. Let us assume that a high-traffic site linked to a page on yours, which is why most of the traffic will be directed to this particular page. In this case, it would make sense to cache only this page. Another good candidate for caching is a page that is expensive to generate, so you would only want it to be generated once every five minutes or so. The tag cloud page in our application fits the latter case. Every time the page is requested, Django iterates through all tags in the database and counts the number of bookmarks for each tag. This is an expensive operation because it requires a large number of database queries. Therefore, caching this view is a good idea.

To cache the `tag_cloud_page` view, you simply apply a decorator called `cache_page` on it. Try this by editing the `bookmarks/views.py` file as highlighted in the following code:

```
from django.views.decorators.cache import cache_page
@cache_page(60 * 15)
def tag_cloud_page(request):
[...]
```

Using the `cache_page` decorator is straightforward. It takes the expiration duration in seconds and lets you specify which views to cache. The rules mentioned in site caching also apply to view caching. If the view receives GET or POST parameters, Django won't cache it.

With this information we finish the section. Caching won't be necessary when you first release your web site to the public. But when your web site grows, or if you suddenly receive a surge of high traffic, the caching system will certainly become handy. So keep it in mind while monitoring the performance of your application.

Next, we are going to learn about the Django testing framework. Testing can sometimes be a tedious task. Wouldn't it be great if you could run a single command that took care of testing your site? Django lets you do this, and we will learn about it in the next section.

Unit testing

During the course of this book, we sometimes had to modify a view that we wrote previously. This actually happens quite often while developing software. One may modify or even rewrite a function to change implementation details, or because the requirements have changed, or simply to re-factor the code and make it more readable.

When you modify a function, you have to test it again to make sure that your changes didn't introduce bugs. However, testing will become a boring task if you have to repeat the same tests every time you modify a function. You may also forget to test all aspects of the function if they are not well-documented. Clearly, this is not an ideal situation. We definitely need a better mechanism to handle testing.

Fortunately, a solution for this already exists. It is called unit testing. The idea is that you write code to test your code. The testing code calls your functions and verifies that they behave as expected, and then prints a report of the results. You only have to write the testing code once. Later, whenever you want to test, you simply run the testing code and examine the resulting report.

Python comes with a framework for unit testing. It is located in the `unittest` module. Django extends this framework to add support for view testing. We will learn how to use the Django unit testing framework in this section.

The test client

In order to interact with views, Django provides a class that emulates browser functionality. You can use it to send requests to your application and receive the responses. Let's learn about it by using the interactive console. Launch the console using this command:

```
$ python manage.py shell
```

Import the `Client` class, create a `Client` object, and retrieve the homepage of the application using a GET request.

```
>>> from django.test.client import Client
>>> client = Client()
>>> response = client.get('/')
>>> print response
Vary: Accept-Language, Cookie
Content-Type: text/html; charset=utf-8
Content-Language: en-us
[... more headers ...]

    <!DOCTYPE html PUBLIC "-//W3C//DTD XHTML 1.0 Transitional//EN"
      "http://www.w3.org/TR/xhtml1/DTD/xhtml1-transitional.dtd">
    <html>
    <head>
      <title>Django Bookmarks |
        Welcome to Django Bookmarks</title>
    [... more HTML ...]
```

Try to send a POST request to the login view. The output will vary depending on whether you provide correct credentials or not.

```
>>> print client.post('/login/', {        'username': 'user',
'password': 'password'})
```

Finally, if there is a view that is restricted to logged-in users only, you can log in using a username and password like this:

```
>>> client.login(username='your_username',

    password='your_password')
```

As you can see from the interactive session, the Client class provides three methods:

- get sends a GET request to a view and takes the URL of the view as a parameter. You can pass an optional dictionary of GET variables to this method.

- post sends a POST request to a view, and takes the URL of the view and a dictionary of POST variables as parameters.

- login simulates the action of logging into the authentication system, and takes the username and password as named arguments.

The Client class is stateful, which means that it retains its state across requests. Once you log in, the later requests will be handled while you are logged in.

The response object returned by the methods of Client contains the following attributes:

- status_code: The HTTP status of the response.
- content: The body of response page.
- template: The Template instance used to render the page. If multiple templates were used, this attribute would be a list of Template objects.
- context: The Context object used to render the template.

Next, we will see whether these fields are useful in checking the succees or failure of the test.

Feel free to experiment more with the Client class. It's important to understand how the Client class works before you move onto the next subsection, in which we will create our first unit test.

Testing the registration view

Now that you are comfortable with the `Client` class, let's write our first test. Unit tests should reside in a module named `tests.py` inside the application folder. Each test should be a method in a class derived from `django.test.TestCase`. The name of the method must start with the word **test**. With this in mind, we will write a test method that tries to register a new user account. Create a file named `tests.py` inside the `bookmarks` directory, and type the following content into it:

```python
from django.test import TestCase
from django.test.client import Client

class ViewTest(TestCase):
  def setUp(self):
    self.client = Client()

  def test_register_page(self):
    data = {
      'username': 'test_user',
      'email': 'test_user@example.com',
      'password1': 'pass123',
      'password2': 'pass123'
    }
    response = self.client.post('/register/', data)
    self.assertRedirects(response, '/register/success/')
```

Let's go through the code line by line:

1. We imported the `TestCase` and `Client` classes.
2. We defined a class called `ViewTest` that was derived from the `TestCase` class. As I said earlier, all the test classes must be derived from this base class.
3. We defined a method called `setUp`. This method is called when the testing process starts. Here we created a `Client` object.
4. We defined a method called `test_register_page`. The name of the method starts with the word test, indicating that it is a test method. The method sends a POST request to the registration view and checks the response—a redirection to the success page.

We checked the response object using a method called `assertRedirects`. This method is inherited from the `TestCase` class. It raises an exception if the response is not a redirection to a particular URL. If an exception is raised, the testing framework knows that the test failed. But if no exception is raised, it assumes that the test succeeded.

The `TestCase` class provides a set of methods to be used in testing. Here is a list of the important ones:

- `assertEqual` expects two values to be equal
- `assertNotEquals` expects two values to be unequal
- `assertTrue` expects a value to be `True`
- `assertFalse` expects a value to be `False`
- `assertRedirects` expects a response to redirect to a particular URL
- `assertContains` expects a response to contain a particular piece of text

The first four methods accept an optional argument called `msg`. If the assertion fails, this argument will be printed along with the error message. This can be particularly useful if you want to provide more information on what failed. We will see an example of this later.

Now that you understand the test class, let's run the actual test by issuing this command:

```
$ python manage.py test bookmarks
```

The output will be similar to the following:

```
Creating test database...
Creating table auth_permission
Creating table auth_group
Creating table auth_user
Creating table auth_message
[...]
...............
-------------------------------------------
Ran 1 test in 0.120s

OK
Destroying test database...
```

What has happened here? The testing framework starts by creating a test database with tables similar to those in the real database. Next, it runs the tests found in the `tests` module. Finally, it prints a report of the results and destroys the test database.

Here, our single test succeeded. To see what the output would be like if the test fails, modify the `test_register_page` view in the `tests.py` file by removing a required form field:

```
def test_register_page(self):
    data = {
        'username': 'test_user',
        'email': 'test_user@example.com',
        'password1': '1',
```

```
        # 'password2': '1'
    }
    response = self.client.post('/register/', data)
    self.assertRedirects(response, '/register/success/')
```

Now run the `python manage.py test bookmarks` command again to see
the results.

```
==============================================================
FAIL: test_register_page (django_bookmarks.bookmarks.tests.ViewTest)
--------------------------------------------------------------
Traceback (most recent call last):
  File "django_bookmarks/bookmarks/tests.py", line 19, in
  test_register_page
    self.assertRedirects(response, '/register/success/')
AssertionError: Response didn't redirect as expected: Response code
was 200 (expected 302)

--------------------------------------------------------------
Ran 1 test in 0.170s
FAILED (failures=1)
```

Our test is working! Django detected an error and gave us the exact details of what
happened. Don't forget to return the test to its original form once done.

Now let's write another test, which is slightly more advanced, to understand the
testing framework better.

Testing the bookmark_save view Now, we will add another testing method to the
`ViewTest` class. This time we will try to log in to a user account, post a bookmark,
and verify that the bookmark appears on the user's page. Open the `bookmarks/
tests.py` file and append the following method to the `ViewTest` class (replacing
`your_username` and `your_password` with your actual credentials):

```
class ViewTest(TestCase):
  [...]
  def test_bookmark_save(self):
    response = self.client.login(
      username='your_username',
      password='your_password'
    )
    self.assertTrue(response, msg='Failed to login.')

    data = {
      'url': 'http://www.example.com/',
      'title': 'Test URL',
      'tags': 'test-tag'
```

```
    }
    response = self.client.post('/save/', data)
    self.assertRedirects(response, '/user/your_username/')
    response = self.client.get('/user/your_username/')
    self.assertContains(
      response,
      'http://www.example.com/'
    )
    self.assertContains(response, 'Test URL')
    self.assertContains(response, 'test-tag')
```

This method does the following three related tests:

- Since the bookmark_save view requires logging in, the method starts by calling login on the Client object, and verifies that logging in was successful. If the login operation fails, the message 'Failed to login' will be printed along with the error message.

- Next, the method tries to save a bookmark by sending a POST request to the bookmark_save view. It verifies that the request succeeded, by checking for a redirect URL.

- Lastly, the method retrieves the user page using a GET request and verifies that the new bookmark appears on it.

If you try the test, it will fail with the following message:

```
==================================================================
FAIL: test_bookmark_save (django_bookmarks.bookmarks.tests.ViewTest)
------------------------------------------------------------------
Traceback (most recent call last):
  File "django_bookmarks/bookmarks/tests.py", line 26, in
  test_bookmark_save
    self.assertTrue(response)
AssertionError

------------------------------------------------------------------
Ran 2 tests in 0.216s

FAILED (failures=1)
```

The method failed to log in, but why? As we saw in the output of the previous test, Django creates a separate database for testing. The contents of the real database are not transferred to the test database. As a result, the tests are run on an empty database. Therefore, the new test method fails to log in, as the database does not contain any users.

To solve this, we will make use of a Django feature called **fixtures**. This feature allows us to automatically insert content into a database when it is created.

To use fixtures, we will first dump the contents of the real database into a text file. Run the following command to do so:

```
$ python manage.py dumpdata bookmarks auth > test_data.json
```

This command exports the tables of the bookmarks and auth applications to a file. Next, add the highlighted line to the `ViewTest` class in the `bookmarks/tests.py` file:

```
class ViewTest(TestCase):
    fixtures = ['test_data.json']
    [...]
```

And this should be it. Now when you run the `python manage.py test` command, Django will create a test database, load the data of `test_data.json` into it, and then run the test methods. The test should have succeeded this time, which means that everything is working as expected.

There are many other scenarios for which you can write unit tests, such as to:

- Check whether registration fails if the two password fields do not match
- Test the "add friend" and "invite friend" views
- Test the "edit bookmark" functionality
- Test that search returns correct results

These are just examples. Writing unit tests to cover as many use cases as possible is important for maintaining a healthy application, and minimizing bugs and regressions. The more unit tests you write, the more confident you can be when your application passes all of the tests. Django makes it extremely easy to unit-test your application. So, make use of this fact.

At some point in the application's life, it will move from the development mode to production. The next section explains how to prepare your Django project for a production environment.

Deploying Django

You have done a lot of work on your web application, and now it is the time to go live. To ensure that the transition from development to production is smooth, there are a number of changes that must be made to the application before it goes live. This section covers these changes to help make the launch of your web application successful.

The production web server

We have been using the development web server that comes with Django throughout this book. Although this server is perfect for the development process, it's definitely not intended to be a production web server because it wasn't developed with security or performance in mind. Therefore, it is certainly not suitable for production.

There are several options to choose from when it comes to the web server, but Apache is by far the most popular choice, and the Django development team actually recommends it. The details of how to set up Django with Apache depend on your hosting solution. Some hosting plans offer pre-configured Django hosting, where you only have to copy your project files to the server, whereas some others give you the freedom to configure everything yourself.

The details of setting up Apache vary depending on a number of factors, and are beyond the scope of this book. If you end up having to configure Apache yourself, consult the Django documentation online at `http://docs.djangoproject.com/en/dev/howto/deployment/modpython/` for detailed instructions.

The production database

So far, we have been using SQLite as our database engine. It is simple and does not require a resident server in memory. SQLite will perform fine in production mode for small web sites. However, it is highly recommended that you switch to a database engine that uses the client/server model in production. As we saw in an earlier chapter, Django supports several database engines, including all the popular ones. The Django team recommends PostgreSQL, but MySQL should be fine as well. Regardless of your choice, you only have to change database options in the `settings.py` file to switch to a different database engine. If you want to use MySQL: create a database, username, and password for Django, and then change the `DATABASE_*` variables accordingly. Everything else remains the same. This is the whole point of the Django database layer.

Turning off debug mode

Whenever an error occurs during development, Django presents a detailed error page with a lot of useful information. However, when you go into production, you don't want your users to see such information. Apart from confusing your users, you risk exposing your web site to security problems if you let strangers see such information.

Turning off debug mode is pretty easy. Open the `settings.py` file, and change the variable `DEBUG` to `False`.

```
DEBUG = False
```

Disabling debug information carries an additional benefit—you improve performance because Django doesn't have to keep track of debug data in order to display it.

Changing configuration variables

There are many configuration variables that need to be created or updated for production. One of them is `Admins`, which holds the names and email addresses of site administrators. You will find it in the `settings.py` file commented out like this:

```
ADMINS = (
    # ('Your Name', 'your_email@domain.com'),
)
```

Insert your name and email here and remove the # symbol to uncomment it and to receive email notifications of code errors when they occur.

Since the email server of your production server most likely differs from your development machine, you may want to update the email configuration variables. Look for the following variables in the `settings.py` file and update them:

- `EMAIL_HOST`
- `EMAIL_PORT`
- `EMAIL_HOST_USER`
- `EMAIL_HOST_PASSWORD`

Also, your web application now has its own domain name. So, you need to update the following settings to reflect this: `SITE_HOST` and `DEFAULT_FROM_EMAIL`.

Finally, if you are using caching, make sure that you have the correct setting in `CACHE_BACKEND` (ideally, `memcached`); you don't want the development backend to be here while you are in production.

Setting error pages

With the debug mode disabled, you should create templates for error pages, particularly these two files:

- `404.html`: This template will be displayed when the requested URL does not exist; in other words, when a page was not found.
- `500.html`: This template will be displayed when an internal server error happens, such as an uncaught exception.

Create these two files with whatever content you like. You can, for example, put a `Page not found` message in the `404.html` template, or a search form. It is recommended that you give these templates a consistent look by deriving them from the base template of your site. Put the templates in the top level of your `templates` folder, and Django will automatically use them.

This should cover the configuration changes that are essential for production. Of course, the section is not exhaustive and there are other settings that you may be interested in. You can, for example, configure Django to notify you via email when a requested page is not found, or provide a list of IP addresses that can see the debug information. For all of this and more, refer to the Django documentation in the `settings.py` file. Hopefully, this section will make your transition from development to production much smoother.

Summary

This chapter covered a variety of interesting topics. We learned about several Django frameworks that are useful when deploying Django. We also learned how to move a Django project from development to a production environment. Notably, the frameworks that we learned about are all very easy to use, so you will be able to effectively utilize them in your future projects.

Here is a quick summary of the Django features explained in this chapter:

- To mark a string for translation, use the `ugettext` or `ugettext_lazy` functions in views, models, and forms, and the `trans` and `blocktrans` template tags in templates.
- To create and compile a language file, use the `makemessages` and `compilemessages` subcommands of `python manage.py`.
- You can globally change the language of the site by creating a configuration variable named `LANGUAGE_CODE` in the `settings.py` file, or per user by enabling the `LocaleMiddleware` class and the `setlanguage` view.
- The caching system allows you to speed up your web site during heavy load. To enable it, choose a caching backend and put it in the `CACHE_BACKEND` variable in the `settings.py` file. Also, set the expiration period in seconds using the `CACHE_MIDDLEWARE_SECONDS` variable in the `settings.py` file.
- To cache your whole site, enable the `UpdateCacheMiddleware` and `FetchFromCacheMiddleware` classes.
- To cache a specific view, use the `cache_page` decorator.

- Unit testing is a framework that allows you to automate tests for your site. Tests should be written in a module named `tests` inside the application package. Test classes should be derived from `django.test.TestCase`. Names of testing methods should start with the word **test**.
- The `Client` class is quite useful for writing tests. It provides three methods—`get` to send a `GET` request, `post` to send a `POST` request, and `login` to authenticate.
- To run tests, issue the command `$ python manage.py test`.

12
What Next?

In this book, we went through the process of building a social bookmarking application from the ground up using Django as our framework. We covered lot of topics related to Web 2.0 and social applications, as well as many Django components. Although the tutorial is finished, there are some Django elements that weren't discussed in the book. This chapter serves as an overview of those elements. It gives only a brief introduction and does not go into the details; but you can always refer to Django's online documentation if you want to learn more about a particular feature or component. The idea behind this chapter is to tell you what is available so that you know what aspect to research if you need to implement a feature that isn't covered in the book.

In this chapter, you will learn about the following Django features:

- Custom template tags and filters
- Model managers and custom SQL
- Generic views
- Some components from the Django standard library

The following are the Web 2.0 features that you can implement into our project:

- Subscription system
- Message system
- User scores

Custom template tags and filters

The Django template system comes with many template tags and filters that make writing templates an easy and flexible job. However, sometimes you may wish to extend the template system with your own tags and filters. This usually happens when you find yourself repeating the same tag structure many times and wish to wrap the structure into a single tag. Or, maybe there is a filter that you want to add to the template system. The pagination system that we wrote in Chapter 9 is a good example of this. Each time we wanted to include the paginator in a page, we had to use the same structure of template tags. It would be cleaner and easier if we could wrap the paginator into a single template tag.

Guess what? Django already allows you to do so, and it is quite easy too! You add a new package to your application called `templatetags`, and put modules that contain tags and filters in it. Let's learn about this by adding a filter that capitalizes a string. Add a folder called `templatetags` to the `bookmarks` folder, and put an empty file called `__init__.py` in it so that Python treats the folder as a package. Now create a module called `bookmarks_filters` in it. We are going to write our filter in this module. Here is an illustration of the directory structure:

```
django_bookmarks/
  bookmarks/
    templatetags/
      __init__.py
      bookmarks_filters.py
```

Now add the following code to the `bookmarks_filters.py` file:

```
from django import template

register = template.Library()

@register.filter
def capitalize(value):
  return value.capitalize()
```

`register` is an object that can be used to introduce new tags and filters to the template system. Here we used the `register.filter` decorator to add the function `capitalize` as a filter.

To use the new filter from within a template, put the following line at the beginning of your template file:

```
{% load bookmarks_filters %}
```

Now you can use the new filter just like any other filter offered by Django:

```
Hi {{ name|capitalize }}!
```

Adding custom template tags works in a way similar to filters. Basically, you define methods to process the tag, and then register the tag to make it available to templates. However, the process is slightly more involved because tags can be more complicated than filters. Further information about custom template tags is available in the Django online documentation.

Model managers and custom SQL

The Django model and database APIs are very powerful. We used them to construct a variety of query sets throughout the book. Mostly, these APIs will be sufficient for your needs. However, there are times when the task at hand requires raw SQL power. For example, you may want to use SQL aggregate functions such as sum or avg to obtain certain types of information from the database. The database layer of Django does not provide methods that offer similar functionality to aggregate functions at the time of writing. To overcome this, Django enables you to send raw SQL to your database for such special situations.

To send SQL queries to the database in Django, use the following code:

```
from django.db import connection
query = '-- SQL code goes here. --'
cursor = connection.cursor()
cursor.execute(query)
```

If you use a SELECT query, you can retrieve the returned rows using:

```
rows = cursor.fetchall()
```

rows is a list of rows. Each row is a list of values that map to columns in the SELECT query. You can use a normal for loop to iterate through the returned rows.

You need to take extra caution while working with raw SQL as it may introduce security or performance issues. In general, avoid using SQL unless you absolutely have to. If the query is built from variables, the execute method provides a way to escape those variables to avoid SQL injection. Use the format sequence %s to indicate the positions of the variables in the query, and then pass the variables in a tuple as the second argument to execute. Here is an example:

```
cursor.execute(
    'SELECT * FROM auth_user WHERE username = %s '
    'AND password = %s', (username, email)
)
```

Never use the string formatting operator % or the string concatenation to build queries—they do not escape variables and will open your application to attacks. Also, there is no need to surround the formatting sequence %s with quotation marks; `execute` does it for you.

To keep your code organized, it's a good idea to wrap your custom SQL queries into a manager for your data model. If you remember from Chapter 3, the `objects` attribute available in data models is known as the manager of the data model. Django lets you customize this manager by adding more methods to it. This is done by deriving a class from the `models.Manager` base class. Therefore, if you want to use raw SQL in a project, read about custom managers in the online documentation and then write one to wrap your SQL queries in it.

Generic views

While working with Django, you will notice that there are certain types of views that are always needed regardless of the project you are working on. For this reason, Django comes with a set of views that can be used in any project. These views are known as generic views and we actually used one of them in a previous chapter. Remember the `direct_to_template` view that renders a template into a page? This view is one example of generic views.

Django offers generic views for the following purposes:

- Create simple views for tasks such as redirecting to another URL or rendering a template.

- List view and detail view for displaying objects from a data model. These views are similar to how the admin page displays list and detail pages for the data models.

- Views to generate date-based archive pages. These can be particularly useful for blogs.

- Views for creating, editing, and deleting objects in data models.

To use one of these views, you import it from `django.views.generic` and then map the view to a URL. You usually need to pass additional arguments as a dictionary to the view in the URL entry. The arguments depend on the view. For example, the `direct_to_template` view takes the template name as an argument.

Whether to use generic views or not is up to you. Some of the views developed in this book could be rewritten using generic views. If you believe that these views can help you in your projects, you will find further information about them in the online documentation.

Contributed sub-frameworks

The `django.contrib` package contains Django's standard library. We have used the following sub-frameworks from this package during earlier chapters in this book:

- `admin`: The Django admin interface
- `auth`: The user authentication system
- `sessions`: The Django session framework
- `syndication`: The feed generation framework

These sub-frameworks greatly simplified our work, whether we were creating registration and authentication facilities, building an administration page, or providing feeds for our content. The `django.contrib` package is a very important part of Django. Knowing its sub-packages and how to use them will save you a lot of time and effort.

This section will provide you with a brief introduction to other frameworks from this package. You won't get into the details of how to use each framework, but you will learn enough to know when to use the framework. Once you want to use a framework in a project, you can read the online documentation to learn more about it.

Flatpages

Web applications may contain pages that are static in nature. For example, your web site may include a set of help pages that rarely change. Django provides an application called **flatpages** to serve static pages. The application is pretty simple. It provides you with a data model to store various bits of information about each page, including the following:

- URL
- Title
- Content
- Template name
- Whether registration is required to view the page

To use the application, you simply enable it in the `INSTALLED_APPS` variable in the `settings.py` file, and add its middleware to `MIDDLEWARE_CLASSES`. After that, you can store and manage your static pages by using a data model provided by the `flatpages` application.

Sites

Django provides a framework called `sites` for managing and running multiple web applications inside a single Django instance. This can be quite useful in many scenarios, such as the following:

- Your web site includes multiple domains or sub-domains, and you want to share the data models across the sites
- You want to offer a subdomain for each one of your users and use the same project for all the sites

The sites framework includes a data model that lets you store all the domains that are managed by the current Django instance. Furthermore, it lets you define a settings file for each domain. This enables you to easily decide what is shared across sites and what is unique to each site.

Markup filters

Many web sites (such as Wikipedia) enable users to enter content in a special markup. This feature offers two benefits:

- The markup is easier to use than HTML, so the users can learn it faster
- The markup is more restricted than HTML, so the users cannot abuse the feature by embedding JavaScript code into the content or perform any other malicious actions

Designing and developing an easy and efficient markup system is not a simple task. Fortunately, there are several markup systems that are commonly used in web applications and at the same time are supported by Django through the markup application. This application adds template filters to process special markup into HTML. Markup languages currently supported by the markup application are as follows:

- Textile
- Markdown
- reStructuredText

Humanize

The humanize application offers a set of filters to add a human touch to your pages. Here is a list of the available filters:

- `apnumber`: For numbers 1 to 9 it returns the number spelled out. Otherwise, it returns the number. In other words, 1 becomes 'one', whereas 10 remains 10.

- `intcomma`: Takes an integer and converts it into a string with a comma between every three digits.

- `intword`: Converts an integer into an easy-to-read form. For example, 1000000, becomes '1.0 million'.

- `ordinal`: Converts an integer to its ordinal form. 1 becomes '1st' and so on.

- `naturalday`: Returns "today", "tomorrow", "yesterday", or a formatted date string.

Sitemaps

Sitemaps is a framework for generating sitemaps, which are XML files that help search engine indexers find dynamic pages on your site. It tells the indexer how important a page is and how often it changes. This information makes the indexing process more accurate and efficient.

The sitemaps framework lets you express the above information in Python code, and then generates an XML document that represents the sitemap of your site.

Cross-Site Request Forgery protection (CSRF)

We discussed how to prevent two types of web attacks in Chapter 5, namely SQL injection and cross site scripting. Django provides protection against another type of attack called **cross-site request forgery**. In this attack, a malicious site tries to manipulate your application by tricking a user who is logged into your web site into opening a specially-crafted page. This page usually contains a JavaScript code that tries to submit a form to your web site. CSRF protection works by embedding a token (that is secret code) into all forms, and verifying the token when the form is submitted. This effectively makes CSRF attacks infeasible.

To activate CSRF protection, you just need to add `'django.contrib.csrf.middleware.CsrfMiddleware'` to MIDDLEWARE_CLASSES, and this will work transparently to prevent CSRF attacks.

This covers the most commonly used sub-frameworks from the `django.contrib` package. The package, which also contains additional applications that are not as important as the ones above, is updated from time to time with new applications. To learn about any application from the `django.contrib` package, you can always read its documentation that's available online.

Message system

Our application allows users to add each other as friends and monitor friend bookmarks. Although these two forms of communication are related to the nature of our bookmarking application, sometimes users want the flexibility of sending private messages to each other. This feature is especially useful for enhancing the social aspect of our web site.

The message system can be implemented in a variety of ways. It can be as simple as providing each user with a contact form, which works by sending its content to the user's email when it is submitted. You already have all of the information needed to build the components of this functionality:

- A message form with a text field for the subject, and a text area for the body of the message
- A view that displays the message form of a user and sends the contents of the form to the user via the `send_mail` function

When allowing users to send emails via your site, you need to be careful in order to prevent abuse of the feature. Here you can restrict contact forms only to the logged-in users or friends.

Another approach to implement the message system is storing and managing messages in the database. This way, users can send and view messages using our application itself instead of using email. Though this approach is more bound to our application, and therefore keeps users on our web site, it involves more work to be implemented. As in the previous approach, you already have all the information needed to implement this approach. The components needed here are as follows:

- A data model for storing messages. It should contain fields for the sender, recipient, subject, and body. You can also add fields for the date, read status, and so on.
- A form for creating messages. Fields for the subject and body are needed.
- A view for listing available messages.
- A view for displaying messages.

This is just one way to implement the message system. For example, you can join the listing and message views into a single view, or provide a view to display sent messages in addition to received ones. The possibilities are numerous, and depend on how advanced you want the features to be.

Subscription system

We offer several web feeds that enable users to monitor updates on our web site. However, some users may still prefer the old way of monitoring updates via email. For those users, you may want to implement an email subscription system into the application. For example, you can let users receive notifications when a bookmark is posted by a friend, or when a bookmark is posted under a certain tag. Furthermore, you can group such notifications and send them in batches to avoid sending large numbers of emails.

The implementation details of this feature greatly depend on how you want it to work. It can be as simple as a data model that stores the tags that each user is subscribed to. It would have a loop that goes through all users who are subscribed to a particular tag and sends notifications to them when a bookmark is posted under this tag. This approach, however, is too basic and generates a lot of emails. A more sophisticated approach may involve storing notifications in a data model and sending them in one email on a daily basis.

User scores

Some web sites (such as `Slashdot.org` and `reddit.com`) track the activity of users by assigning a score to each user. This score is incremented whenever the user contributes to the web site in some way. User scores can be utilized in a variety of ways. For example, you can release new features to your most active users first, or provide other advantages to active users, which will motivate other users to contribute more to your web site.

Implementing the user scores is pretty simple. You need a data model to maintain scores in the database. After that, you can use the Django model API to access and manipulate scores from within views.

Summary

The purpose of this chapter is to prepare you for tasks that were not covered in the book. It provided introductions to numerous topics. You read about creating custom template tags and filters, using raw SQL queries and generic views. You also learned about several Django sub-frameworks. These included Flatpages for serving static content, sites for hosting multiple web sites in one Django instance, Sitemaps for exporting a search engine map, and several useful template filters. When a need arises for a certain feature, you now know where to look in order to find a framework that helps you implement the feature quickly and cleanly.

The chapter also gave some ideas that you may want to implement into the bookmarking application. The ideas included a message system, a subscription system, and tracking user activity with scores. Working on these features will give you more opportunities to experiment with Django and extend your knowledge of its frameworks and inner workings.

Index

Packt Open Source Project Royalties

When we sell a book written on an Open Source project, we pay a royalty directly to that project. Therefore by purchasing Django 1.0 Web Site Development, Packt will have given some of the money received to the Django Project.

In the long term, we see ourselves and you—customers and readers of our books—as part of the Open Source ecosystem, providing sustainable revenue for the projects we publish on. Our aim at Packt is to establish publishing royalties as an essential part of the service and support a business model that sustains Open Source.

If you're working with an Open Source project that you would like us to publish on, and subsequently pay royalties to, please get in touch with us.

Writing for Packt

We welcome all inquiries from people who are interested in authoring. Book proposals should be sent to author@packtpub.com. If your book idea is still at an early stage and you would like to discuss it first before writing a formal book proposal, contact us; one of our commissioning editors will get in touch with you.

We're not just looking for published authors; if you have strong technical skills but no writing experience, our experienced editors can help you develop a writing career, or simply get some additional reward for your expertise.

About Packt Publishing

Packt, pronounced 'packed', published its first book "Mastering phpMyAdmin for Effective MySQL Management" in April 2004 and subsequently continued to specialize in publishing highly focused books on specific technologies and solutions.

Our books and publications share the experiences of your fellow IT professionals in adapting and customizing today's systems, applications, and frameworks. Our solution-based books give you the knowledge and power to customize the software and technologies you're using to get the job done. Packt books are more specific and less general than the IT books you have seen in the past. Our unique business model allows us to bring you more focused information, giving you more of what you need to know, and less of what you don't.

Packt is a modern, yet unique publishing company, which focuses on producing quality, cutting-edge books for communities of developers, administrators, and newbies alike. For more information, please visit our website: www.PacktPub.com.

Django 1.0 Template Development

ISBN: 978-1-847195-70-8   Paperback: 252 pages

A practical guide to Django template development with custom tags, filters, multiple templates, caching, and more

1. Dive into Django's template system and build your own template

2. Learn to use built-in tags and filters in Django 1.0

3. Practical tips for project setup and template structure

4. Use template techniques to improve your application's performance

Expert Python Programming

ISBN: 978-1-847194-94-7   Paperback: 350 pages

Best practices for designing, coding, and distributing your Python software

1. Learn Python development best practices from an expert, with detailed coverage of naming and coding conventions

2. Apply object-oriented principles, design patterns, and advanced syntax tricks

3. Manage your code with distributed version control

4. Profile and optimize your code

5. Proactive test-driven development and continuous integration

Please check **www.PacktPub.com** for information on our titles

Lightning Source UK Ltd.
Milton Keynes UK
UKOW020337300612

195201UK00003B/133/P